KEYBOARD
Instruments

Clive Unger-Hamilton

KEYBOARD *Instruments*

PHAIDON

First published in Great Britain by
Phaidon Press Limited,
Littlegate House,
St Ebbe's Street, Oxford OX1 1SQ
ISBN: 0 7148 2177 2

Art Director
Nicholas Eddison
Designer
Gillian Della Casa
Picture Editor
Celia Dearing
Picture Researcher
Liz Hart
Research Assistant
Jane Greening
Production Manager
Kenneth Cowan
Production Editor
Fred Gill
Editorial Assistant
Sue Brown

Filmset by Facet Filmsetting Ltd,
Southend-on-Sea, England
Illustrations originated by
Hongkong Graphic Arts, Hong Kong
Printed and bound by Dai Nippon,
Hong Kong

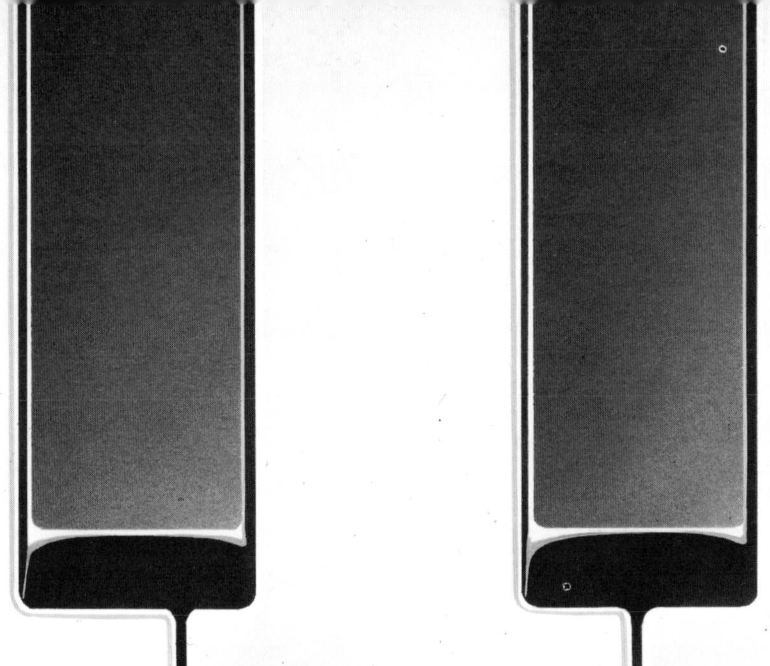

CONTENTS

FOREWORD

A hundred years ago, the most likely way to hear music was by listening to someone play the piano. There would be an instrument in every cottage parlour, village chapel and dockside saloon. The reason for this was its unique versatility as an instrument. When necessary, it could take on the role of an entire orchestra: until the First World War, when the gramophone had made its impact, people knew the symphonic repertoire almost exclusively through arrangements for the piano.

The instrument's popularity meant that its repertoire was extremely extensive. Yet those who see the piano as the only keyboard instrument are cutting themselves off from vast riches. Pianos have been in mass production for less than two hundred years: keyboard history and the repertoire extend back for centuries before that. The organ is thought of too often as the lacklustre accompaniment to church services, and the harpsichord noticed only as a background to television commercials. It is possible to be as emotionally stirred by an Elizabethan galliard played on the virginals as by a Chopin nocturne on a modern concert grand.

Keyboard Instruments sets out, in the first part of the book, to explain how the different families arose, co-existed and evolved. The sudden death of the harpsichord at the end of the eighteenth century and its renaissance in our own time is a particularly interesting phenomenon. How technology has affected the music written for the instruments is another fascinating study that is too rarely given its due.

Part two deals with the music written for the organ, harpsichord, clavichord and piano over the last five hundred years. In the space available, it is impossible to include every work; but I hope the reader will find a cogent thread of musical development in the composers and pieces of music selected for discussion. Chamber music involving keyboard instruments has, unfortunately, had to be omitted from this survey for reasons of space. Jazz also has been left out of this section, not for any personal preference, but because so little of it is available for the average pianist to buy and study for himself.

The last part of *Keyboard Instruments* is a reference section. It consists, in the main, of biographical sketches of one hundred virtuosos familiar from record, radio or concert hall. Also included are a handful of nineteenth-century figures, who, while unavailable for us to hear even on disc, have made an important impact on one or another aspect of their art. Jazz pianists are also included here.

An 18th-century French instrument-maker's workshop, from Diderot's *Encyclopédie*

The Instruments

The first section of this book is concerned with the instruments themselves: how they work, how they evolved, and what is or has been their place in society. It subdivides into three shorter groups, one on each family of keyboard instruments: plucked (the harpsichord, spinet and virginals), blown (the organ family) and struck (the piano and clavichord). The mechanics and working of the instruments are shown diagrammatically where possible, and supporting illustration has been used to attempt to set the instruments in their historical context. But before this, we must examine the function, origin and remarkable design of the keyboard itself, bearing in mind that no amount of reading about music can ever take the place of intelligent listening. To this end, the reader is referred to numerous recordings recommended within the text of Parts II and III of the book that are intended to supplement the information within this section.

The function of the keyboard is to enable the player to control as many notes as possible with his ten fingers. He has, of course, a great advantage over other musicians: unlike the violinist, for example, who has to create and pitch every note he plays, on a keyboard the notes are made for him – whether by strings, reeds or pipes.

To facilitate covering the maximum number of notes (and the compass of an octave must be playable by each hand), a compromise is necessary. The number of notes in the scale is reduced to twelve. F♯ is made to substitute for G♭ when necessary, G♯ for A♭ and so on. The alternative to thus putting every note fractionally out of tune would be to have virtually twice as many notes between the octave. Various methods of doing this have been tried: by splitting the black keys laterally (or lengthwise), for example, but the results are costly – and extremely difficult to manipulate in pieces of any complexity.

The first recognizable keyboards appear to have arisen in the thirteenth and fourteenth centuries, though there is a persistent legend that ascribes its invention to the medieval theoretician Guido d'Arezzo. Perhaps the shape even evolved from little T-shaped keys that stop the strings of the hurdy-gurdy. Sharps and flats (the so-called 'black' notes) were added gradually, in the same way as the intervals and chords they created came to be aesthetically acceptable. B♭ was the first to be added: since the white-note scale was the main one, the black note was added to remove the discordant intervals produced by B♮. So, by degrees, the keyboard filled out, until it was complete by about the middle of the fifteenth century.

The very early instruments were small, and only had a narrow range of notes. By the early sixteenth century, they had expanded from about two and a half octaves up to four, while most eighteenth-century music, Scarlatti or Mozart for example, requires a five-octave compass. Organs, of course, tended to have a somewhat shorter range, since many of the lower notes were given to the pedals, a separate keyboard for the feet.

People are often confused by the reversal of the colouring on older keyboards. This has no significance apart from various provincial conventions or personal idiosyncrasy. Indeed, there are many examples of exotic substances such as tortoiseshell being used for this.

d
c
d.
Fig

THE SOCIAL HISTORY

'He is verye often drunke and by means thereof he hathe by unorderlye playing on the organs putt the quire out of time and disordered them.' That renaissance complaint, preserved in Lincoln Cathedral, underlines the importance of the organ in a time where belief in God was universal. The Church was the main social focus, for there was little entertainment either inside or outside the home. People looked forward to attending a service: they went there to gossip, to gamble and – as at St Paul's Cathedral – to sell cabbages, books or whatever else was in demand.

After the austerity of medieval devotional excesses, during which instrumental music was not available, the organ – when it finally achieved ecclesiastical status – ensured that at least some of the congregation were encouraged to worship rather than divert themselves.

The instruments built during the baroque era bear testimony to the veneration in which the organ was held. Music lovers would walk miles to hear great masters perform: Bach himself walked 200 miles to hear old Buxtehude at Lübeck. But organs were then costly to build, and to install. Outside the Church, where their provenance was funded by rich penitents as insurance against the Day of Judgement, only the very wealthy could afford to possess such an instrument in their private chapels. It was in the nineteenth century, with the evolution of the harmonium, that organ sound became available to domestic users. With foot-operated bellows (suitably mouse-proofed) and with a variety of stops, the instrument was accompaniment to family prayers in many a Victorian household.

The advent of the cinema brought further refinements. Cowbells, train-whistles and raindrops supplied what was lacking before the 'talkies'. Throughout the drama on the screen, the enormous machine stayed in the pit in an accompanying role, then rose up during the interval, in gorgeous purple and gold, to slaughter the audience with the latest dance craze. The 'organ spot' at the local biograph was often the most popular item on the programme. It is only in the last thirty years or so that the

In 17th-century Amsterdam, the **Oude Kerk** was a fashionable place to meet and gossip between services, and morning strollers would be entertained by Sweelinck's organ playing

harpsichord – for so long the standard keyboard instrument – has come back into fashion. In the seventeenth and eighteenth centuries it (or one of its smaller relatives) occupied much the same place in the home that has more recently been relinquished by the upright piano to the television set. What were its virtues then, and why has it been resuscitated?

Its mechanics were simple. It worked by gravity, and without the complex escapement that was to change the face of music in the form of the pianoforte at the end of the eighteenth century. In the baroque period, music was contrapuntal: it was conceived in terms of separate but relatively equal voices. The very clarity of plucked-string tone made the harpsichord family ideally suited to the musical practice of the age. To hear, for example, Bach's Italian Concerto upon the instrument for which it was written, reveals all the inner ingenuities that are blurred by the sweet Romantic furriness of the modern concert grand. The importance of harpsichord music lies as much within the inner and lower voices as in the melody, which began to take the upper hand in the age of Haydn and Mozart.

The volume of harpsichord sound is fairly light. In the seventeenth and early eighteenth centuries there were no concert halls: admission to hear one of the great players of the day, such as Handel or Domenico Scarlatti, was by invitation to one of the grand houses of the period. It was only later, when public recitals became a part of musical life, that the necessary carrying power had to come from an instrument more equipped to cope – the piano.

On a harpsichord, spinet or virginal, whether the instrument is merely touched or struck by the player with all his might, the volume level remains the same. It is to the great Polish musician Wanda Landowska that we owe the renewed interest in the harpsichord. Tired of the mushy, romantic performances of Bach on the piano, Landowska, trained as a pianist herself, commissioned from the Paris firm of Pleyel what she called a 'new-old instrument': a modern copy of the eighteenth-century harpsichord. Not everyone (as she put it) was delighted. Indeed Sir Thomas Beecham, always a traditionalist, likened its sound to that of two skeletons copulating on a tin roof. Others, however, appreciated the new insight which harpsichord performances could give into the works of Bach, Handel, Couperin, Scarlatti and Rameau.

In the last two decades, Wanda Landowska has herself became rather outmoded. At the beginning of the present century, Pleyel used their piano-building techniques to mimic harpsichord sound, complete with iron frame. Today, a more 'authentic' method is used, reconstructing both in materials and dimensions the immense craftsmanship of such early keyboard-builders as Ruckers of Antwerp, Hass of Germany and Kirckman of London. The tone of modern reproductions, compared with the iron-framed, early twentieth-century instruments of Pleyel is, because of their very lightness of construction, slighter yet more resonant than Landowska's instruments.

The harpsichord sound, considered pretty esoteric even a few decades ago, is now so accepted that it has even generated a backlash. Musicians are beginning to play Bach on the piano again – but with that clarity of line, unmuddied by pedal, that the harpsichord has taught them to respect.

Playing the keyboard of a plucked instrument requires quite a different approach from

that of the piano. The sound, for a start, is not on what pianists call the key-bed, but speaks as soon as the instrument is touched. Any unevenness in playing will therefore show up very readily, exacerbated by the instrument's thinness of tone. Whole multitudes of wrong notes can be disguised by the piano's thick, woolly sonority: not so for the indifferent harpsichordist, whose instrument exposes ruthlessly all inaccuracies of rhythm or uncertain fingering.

The approach must be soft (to avoid any ugly wooden thumps when the key hits bottom) yet 'firm as an eagle's claw'. For when all the machinery of the harpsichord is in use (two eight-foot strings and one four-foot), the resistance to the player's touch is substantial. Matters are therefore arranged that the three plucks of a note played occur one after the other in a series of very closely timed intervals. Slow depression of a harpsichord key with all the stops out reveals this point. So harpsichord touch must be fast and exquisitely precise, but gentle enough to avoid the hard knocking that results from playing the keyboard as if it were a percussion instrument. Bach, we are told by his first biographer, Forkel, 'played with so easy and so small a motion of his fingers that it was scarcely perceptible. Only the first joints of the fingers moved: his hand retained, even in the most difficult passages, its rounded form; the fingers rose very little from the keys, hardly more than in a trill, and while one finger was employed, the others remained quietly in position. Still less did the other parts of his body take any share in his playing, as happens with many whose hand is not light enough.' There is much to be learned from studying reports of the great masters in performance, and from contemporary books of instruction. One other anecdote from the period still has the power to thrill: it concerns Domenico Scarlatti, the greatest harpsichordist who ever lived, and is reported of the Irish virtuoso Thomas Roseingrave. Being asked to sit down to the harpsichord and favour the company with a toccata,

The **virginals** accompanying flute and voice; an engraving based on a painting by Crispin de Pass the Younger

'and finding myself in better finger than usual' he did so. After which 'a grave young man, dressed entirely in black, and with a black wig' approached the instrument. Then, says Roseingrave, 'when he began to play, it were as though ten thousand d--ls had been at the instrument; he had never heard such passages of execution and effect before.'

For the last 150 years, the piano has been the very essence of social intercourse and domestic entertainment. Devotional songs, comic ditties and especially ballads of a sentimental nature heaved many a bosom in Georgian and Victorian times, attended by much mutual self-applause.

The piano became infinitely more popular than the harpsichord had ever done. To a great extent, this was made possible by the Industrial Revolution. Iron frames and complex actions could be mass-produced, as opposed to the individual handicrafting involved in every stage of harpsichord manufacture. So the piano became cheaper and more available to the aspirant middle classes that the Industrial Revolution had created, who by 1830 or thereabouts had not only more wealth but much greater ambition than the labouring classes from which they had sprung.

At the same time, the social upheaval that accompanied the industrial restructuring of society bred a spirit of revolution and respect for the individual that was far removed from

A family group round the parlour piano in 1865. Their repertoire might include a few operatic airs, quadrilles, galops and (for Sundays) pianoforte arrangements of Handel choruses. They would be familiar with the music of Wallace, Balfe, Spohr and Bishop, names which are all but forgotten today

the hierarchical system of the eighteenth century. Each man was now allowed to choose his own destiny, and none more so than the tortured musical spirit. By the middle of the nineteenth century there was virtually no parlour without its 12-guinea cottage upright from such prestigious houses as Broadwood, Brinsmead or Chickering. Piano duets (reductions of orchestral favourites), heart-searching airs, quadrilles for dancing or even whole operas were published in simplified editions to bring great music within the range of the most butter-fingered. A whole industry grew up to cater for the new generation of aspiring virtuosos. Songs and piano fantasias were rushed into print with the alacrity that record companies now flood the market with the latest pop singles. Topicality was essential. Christmas would bring a rash of pieces with such seasonal titles as *On the Ice* or *The Merry Sleigh-Ride*; if they had been ready three months earlier, the same pieces might just as easily have been called *Feuille d'automne* or *Tossing the Hay*. To enable the public to cope with the minimal technical demands made by these *oeuvres*, piano methods of a shattering banality were hastily assembled, leading the beginner from *The Bluebells of Scotland* through the *March from 'Scipio'* to Grand Variations on themes like *Home, Sweet Home*.

There were correspondence courses that gave spurious but highly decorative diplomas. At a higher level, the *bona fide* music colleges expanded to include graded examinations at all levels of musicianship. These have done tremendous work in raising the standard of piano teaching to a level far above the tentative tinkling of the mid-nineteenth century.

But it was also the age of the piano virtuoso *par excellence*. Crowds flocked to see the great superstars: Liszt, Thalberg and Clara Schumann were possibly the three supreme pianists of the time, their great talents proving an inspiration that is still valid today.

But programmes in recitals were much less reverent than they are now. Improvisation was a common feature of concerts, as were flashy transcriptions and fantasias on popular operatic airs, for example. This was the pop music of the day. At one charity concert in Paris in 1837, six pianists (including Chopin, Liszt, Thalberg and Beethoven's favourite pupil, Czerny) played a set of six variations on six pianos. The theme was *Suoni la tromba* from Bellini's *I Puritani*: an introduction, finale and cadenzas between the variations were provided (improvised?) by Liszt. He later arranged the work, added an orchestral part, and featured it frequently at concerts later in life.

Though the piano now lacks the status of high-tech stereo equipment, the chances are that it will be restored to its former popularity. The micro-chip and the resulting excess of leisure, further exacerbated by an increased life expectancy, will necessitate creative, practical, human challenges in a multitude of forms. There will be a substantial gap to be filled, once the tradition of the 'dignity of labour' has been recognized for the myth that it is.

THE ORGAN

More than 4000 years ago there were organs that bore an uncanny resemblance to the instruments of today. The wind, however, was supplied by water pressure, and the device was accordingly known as a hydraulis. All that was really lacking was what we know as a conventional keyboard (see p. 10). Later, similar instruments were in use in ancient Rome: the emperor Nero is recorded as having been a skilled performer.

The organ had reached northern Europe before the tenth century. One astonishing instrument recorded at Winchester Cathedral boasted 400 pipes, needed seventy men to blow it and certainly more than one player. Most instruments were much smaller: some were equipped with a single set of flue pipes, and could be played (one-handedly) and blown by the performer – the portative organ.

By degrees, the organ acquired extra ranks of pipes, to give a fuller and more varied sound, and by the fifteenth century some instruments were already fitted with pedals. In the seventeenth century, England suffered a setback: under the Commonwealth, organs were banned as being profane, and many marvellous examples were destroyed.

For many, the great age of the organ was the eighteenth century, virtually because of the work of one man, J. S. Bach. The instrument he used at Weimar, however (where he wrote most of his organ music), was relatively small and insignificant, with extremely awkward pedals.

With the industrial revolution came further developments. The instruments became much larger, with many more ranks of both reed and flue pipes, refinements of the swell mechanism, and higher wind pressure. With this immense growth in size came a related loss in clarity of tone, however, resulting in the thick, washy sound that puts so many people off the beauties of the instrument.

The twentieth century brought electric systems to cope with the delicate tracker mechanism of rods and levers, though today some instruments are built in the earlier manner, in an attempt to reproduce as faithfully as possible the sound and feel of the older instruments. The modern electronic organs, whatever their merits, lie beyond the scope of this book. They are as yet too young to be dignified with a history.

(Above): **A portative organ** being played in procession (1517). *(Right):* The organ played by **Bach** at Arnstadt (*c.* 1650). *(Far right):* American **reed organ**, often called a harmonium. *(Below):* A **theatre organ** (1934) now restored to working order

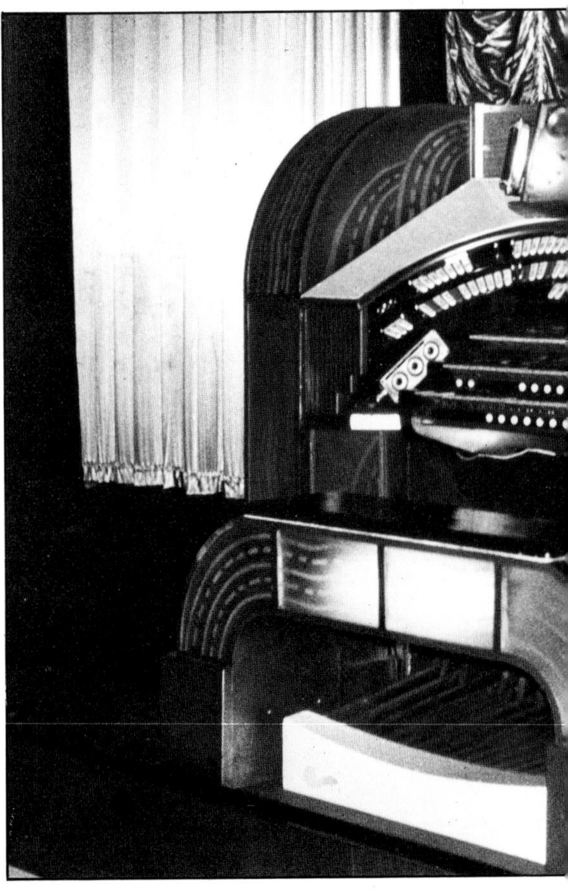

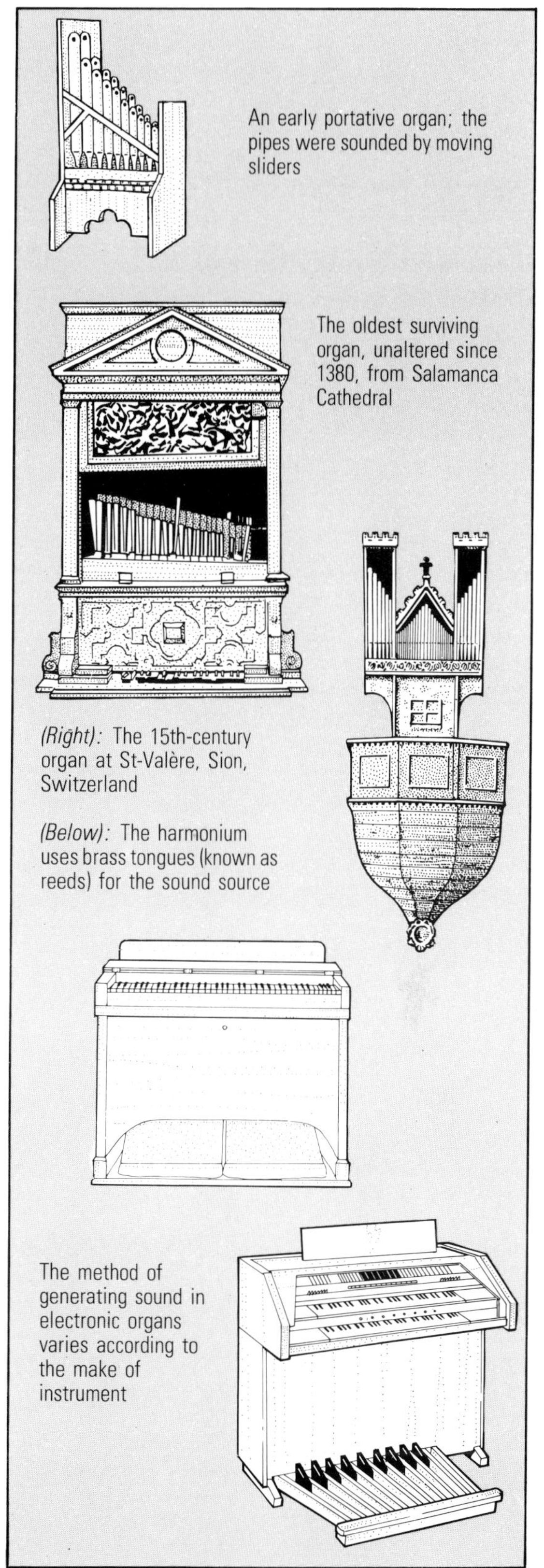

An early portative organ; the pipes were sounded by moving sliders

The oldest surviving organ, unaltered since 1380, from Salamanca Cathedral

(Right): The 15th-century organ at St-Valère, Sion, Switzerland

(Below): The harmonium uses brass tongues (known as reeds) for the sound source

The method of generating sound in electronic organs varies according to the make of instrument

Technically the organ is a wind instrument. It differs from all other wind instruments, however, in that there is a separate pipe for every note: each pipe produces only one sound. Furthermore, because of the organ's construction, the pipe plays at a set volume. To make the instrument play louder, the organist must bring in more pipes (as detailed in the accompanying illustrations).

But there is a way to make the pipes play more quietly. Most organs have more than one keyboard (or 'manual'). In a two-manual instrument, the pipes played from the upper manual are known as the 'swell' organ. They are encased in a box, sometimes the size of a room, the walls of which are shuttered. By using a foot control (the swell pedal), the organist can close the shutters and reduce the sound of the instrument.

The pipes outside the swell box are known as the 'great organ' and are played from the lower manual. Although the great organ includes the largest and most important pipes, such as the diapason, the swell organ often has a much greater variety of voices at its disposal.

Over the last hundred years, electricity has replaced manpower for blowing the organ; and the ponderous 'tracker' action has also been improved by today's technology. Yet much remains the same in the instrument that inspired some of Bach's greatest music. Only the mechanics have changed: musicologists and technicians have taken immense pains to re-create the sound of the baroque organ.

A small church organ and its mechanics. Three different types of pipe can be seen; the diapason pipes, which give the organ its distinctive tone, are usually displayed on the casework *(above)*. Behind the casework stand the conical trumpet pipes, their strident tone given by metal reeds in the pipes themselves. At the back are the box-like, deep-sounding bourdons.

(Left) The cleric pumping this medieval organ is kneeling to allow the organist an uninterrupted view of the choir

Two valves must be opened before air can pass from wind-chest to organ-pipe: the slider, operated from the stop-knobs, and the pallets, linked by trackers to the keyboard. Pressing a key (1) moves the sticker (2), trips the backfall (3), pulls the tracker (4) with its adjusting screw (5), and so opens the spring-held pallet (8) in the windchest (7). Drawing the stop-knob rotates the rollers (6), draws the slider (9) and lines up the holes (10) in the slider with its rank of pipes.

THE HARPSICHORD

For the last two centuries, the piano has been the keyboard instrument *par excellence*, but before that the members of the harpsichord had been dominant for a much longer period. Its sonority dictated the style of the music that was written for it: the most important fact about its sonority is its lack of sustaining power.

Harpsichords have no sustaining pedal (the right-hand pedal on the piano). As soon as the finger releases the key, the note ceases to sound. Accordingly a complex system of prolonging notes was evolved, which also served to accent desired notes, since the instrument is also fairly unresponsive to touch. The system was one of decorating notes with trills, shakes and turns. It is important to remember that the abundance of ornamentation in baroque music is not merely decorative: prolonged trills serve to sustain the sound of a note that would otherwise die away, while short trills, snaps and turns give the necessary accent to strong beats or important notes. This apparent affectation of baroque music must always be seen in the light of its historical function.

A large harpsichord is an expensive and unwieldy instrument (though less so than a piano, thanks to its lighter, wooden frame). For domestic purposes it was large and costly, so many more homes tended to have a spinet. This is a very similar instrument to the harpsichord, but much smaller: the equivalent in today's terms of an upright piano instead of a full-length concert grand. The earlier virginals, a favourite in sixteenth-century England, had however a much more distinctive sound, with a bright treble and a full, round bass.

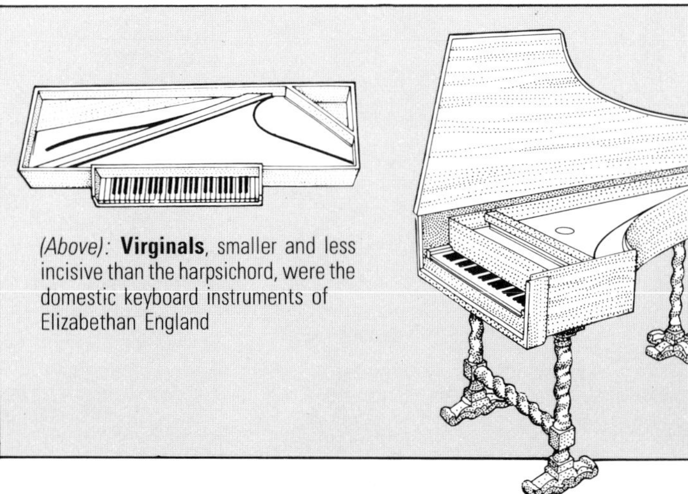

(Above): **Virginals**, smaller and less incisive than the harpsichord, were the domestic keyboard instruments of Elizabethan England

(Left): **Italian harpsichord.** The familiar leg-of-mutton shape had become established by the early 16th century

(Right): **Flemish harpsichord.** Heavier, with more sustaining power than the Italian. Its second row of strings sounding an octave higher gave it a sparkling treble

(Left): An Italian painted **clavicytherium**, or upright harpsichord, 17th century. *(Above):* A rare example of the **double virginals**. The highly decorated casework conceals a drawer containing a second keyboard which can be placed on top of the main instrument. *(Right):* A veneered **English spinet**, from the museum of the Royal College of Music. *(Far right):* A modern **two-manual harpsichord** standing on a pedal harpsichord

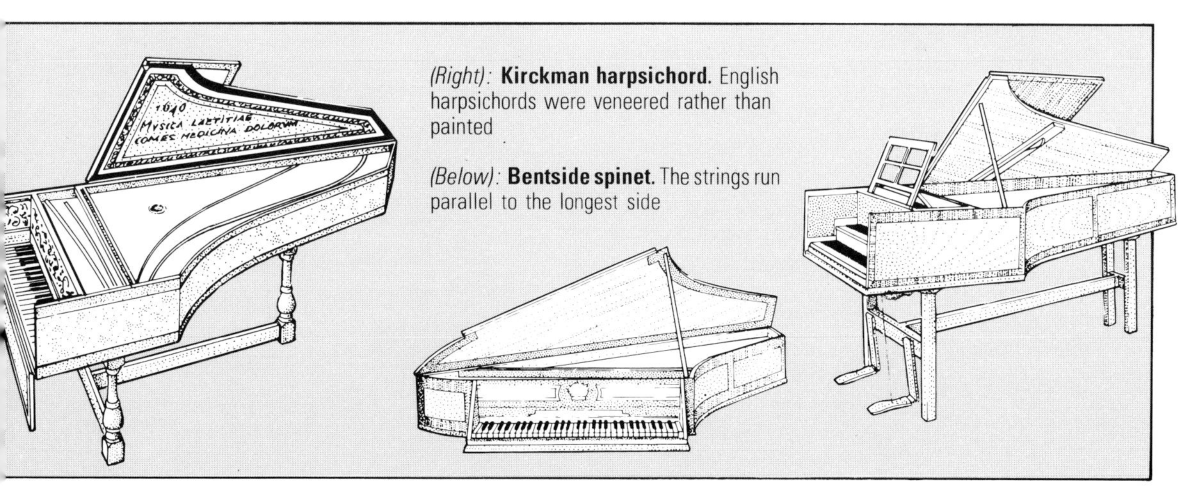

(Right): **Kirckman harpsichord.** English harpsichords were veneered rather than painted

(Below): **Bentside spinet.** The strings run parallel to the longest side

Because the harpsichord family (virginals, spinet and harpsichord) is one of plucked strings, gradations of volume by touch are not possible. Getting louder or softer, therefore, is achieved by using a series of stops – rather like organ stops – that can marshal or discard extra ranks of strings at will.

Basic keyboard tone is said to be at 'eight-foot pitch'. This means that when middle C is played, middle C will sound. On a large, two-manual instrument, the two keyboards (each with its own set of strings at eight-foot pitch) will have slightly different plucking points in which one – generally the upper manual – is of a more pungent, nasal quality. This, by combining two different tonal qualities, gives the effect of a solo voice with accompaniment.

A set of shorter strings can be brought into play – the four-foot register – sounding one octave higher. This adds brilliance to the sound: for loud 'tutti' effects, all three sets of strings can be coupled together, to produce maximum volume. Such instruments probably represented the specification available to the great masters, Bach, Handel and Domenico Scarlatti.

Some of the more outré instruments have gone so far as to add an extra, thicker set of strings pitched one octave below the note struck (the sixteen-foot register), which lends a majestic plangency to the sound. In the baroque era, however, this appears to have been very rare. It was probably devised to compete (unsuccessfully) with the piano. Because of the recent vogue for 'authenticity', the sixteen-foot register has fallen into disfavour. Yet such masters as Landowska, Rafael Puyana and George Malcolm have made on record highly persuasive use of the stop. Perhaps it is that our ears have become so altered by the rich sounds of the nineteenth century and beyond that our musical minds feel a need (consciously or not) for a richer sonority from the harpsichord.

Perhaps it was an earlier desire for variety that evolved the harpsichord's other weapon: the harp stop. This activates a pad of felt across the strings, giving a dry muted effect of great charm that is often used for echo effects. Like the other stops on the instrument, it is brought into play by the use of hand stops or pedals (earlier harpsichords tended to use pedals) which can be seen projecting from above or below the keyboard. Also like the other stops, it is brought into play completely at the discretion of the performer: much of the joy of playing comes from deciding one's own 'orchestration' of each different piece.

The harpsichord illustrated is a single manual instrument with two 'stops' or sets of strings tuned an octave apart. Each key has two jacks, one for each string, which rest on leather pads on the backs of the keys. The upper parts of the jacks are supported by slots in sliding racks. Advancing these racks slightly brings the jacks into play

Pressing the key lifts the jacks (2) causing the plectrum (3) to pluck the string (1). When the key is released, the plectrum tilts back and slides past the string without plucking it. A tiny spring returns the plectrum to its playing position

(Right): A **square piano** in the late Regency style, decorated with elaborate inlay. By John Broadwood, about 1830

(Left): **Giraffe piano**, about 1840. These were of German or Viennese origin. The action was below the keyboard and the instrument often had several 'effects' pedals

(Right): A modern **portable clavichord**. The action is the simplest of any keyboard instrument

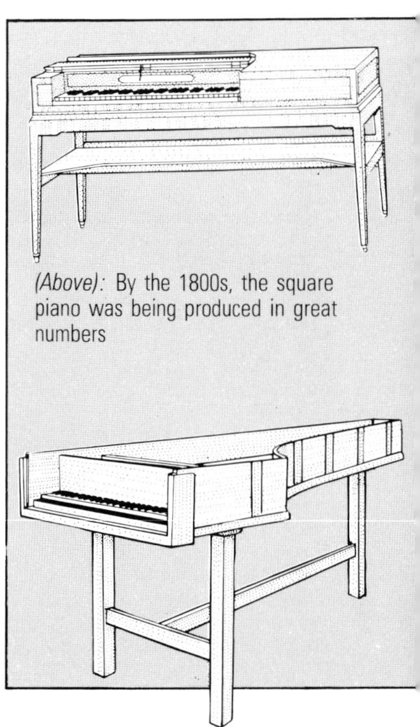

(Above): By the 1800s, the square piano was being produced in great numbers

THE PIANO

In the mid-eighteenth century, the need for a new, simpler music put the keyboard player at a disadvantage. Such music relied largely on 'expression' in performance, and no matter how many stops and colours the harpsichordist had at his disposal, he lacked the ability to shade the melody with sensibility.

There was no problem getting a hammer to strike the string with varying force: the difficulty lay in organizing its rebound. Every percussion player knows that if his hammer lies an instant too long on the playing surface of an instrument, it results in a dull thud without the proper resonance.

When this problem was solved, harpsichord-makers added all kinds of embellishments to compete with the appeal of the fortepiano. Piano-makers responded with some alarming gadgetry of their own: drums the cymbals operated by the feet, for example

But such a fashion was short-lived. In the early nineteenth century, the major design problems of the piano – most importantly, increased sonority and reliable action – were effectively solved. By the time the great virtuosos such as Liszt and Chopin were playing in the European capitals, the instruments they used were only little removed from the pianos we play and hear today.

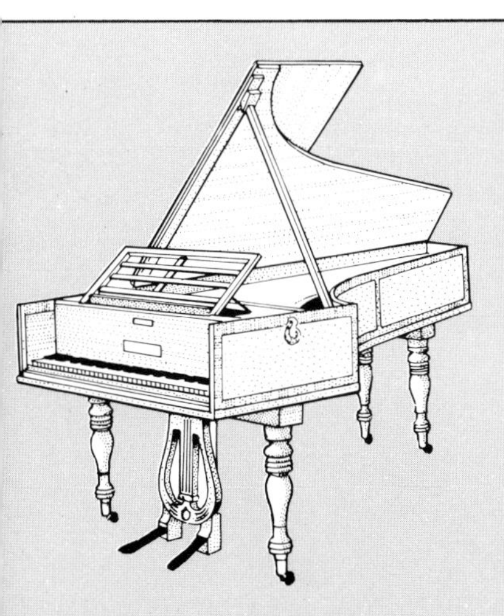

(Left): By Beethoven's time the grand piano's compass had been extended to six octaves, and sustaining pedals were introduced

(Below): Iron frames were introduced into the upright piano from about 1825

(Left): The earliest pianos, made by Cristofori, had a simple piano action fitted into a harpsichord case.

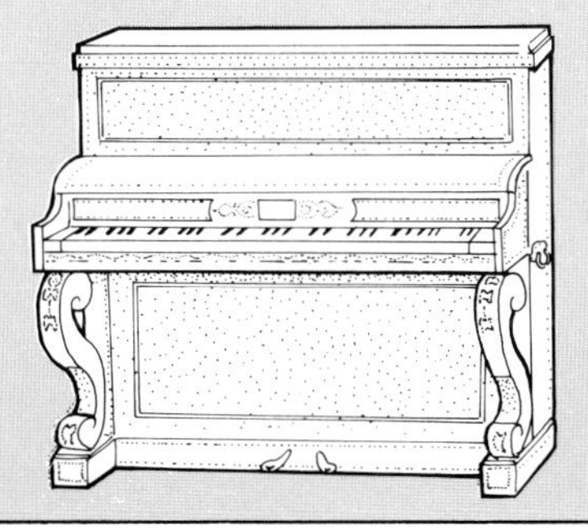

(Above): Some large concert grands are provided with a third pedal which can sustain selected notes

From merely banging a drum to create a sound, it took a major jump to invent a keyboard that would do the work for you. The principle of the clavichord used the primary idea, where one side of a depressed fulcrum rises to bridge a stretched string. But it was capable of infinite subtlety: it could effect a most touching vibrato (known in Germany, where the instrument was most popular, as *Bebung*). The clavichord's tiny sound makes it an ideal domestic instrument, though too weak for the concert hall.

In fact, many of Beethoven's sonatas were published as suitable for harpsichord. But such a description merely demonstrates the publisher's desire to catch as many markets as possible.

The action of Beethoven's piano is essentially the same as that of the modern concert grand. The original problem facing instrument-builders was contriving an 'escapement', so that the hammer could fall back fractionally and allow the string to vibrate. Once this principle was solved (in the eighteenth century), nineteenth-century technology went on to provide much increased sonority. This was thanks principally to the invention of the iron frame, as well as ever more sophisticated damping mechanisms. The invention of the iron frame (for some time a matter of dispute between the firms of Érard and Broadwood) made possible an extended compass for the keyboard, as well as increasing the instrument's ability to hold its tuning. A full-size piano must withstand a string tension of up to 30 tons: the modern concert grand is a mechanical triumph that owes nothing to micro-chip technology.

Essentially, a piano mechanism should be able to produce a gradation of dynamics controlled absolutely by the pressure or force of the fingers on the keys. In practice, this calls for an escapement by which a hammer strikes a string with a variable force, and bounces off again immediately, so as not to interfere with the vibration of the string. In addition each string needs to have a damper which is lifted off the string as long as the key is held down. **Grand piano mechanism:** (1) key; (2) check head; (3) hammer head; (4) hammer shank support; (5) repetition lever; (6) jack; (7) set-off button; (8) damper body; (9) damper

The first piano action. Cristofori's attempt to build an instrument which could play with shaded dynamics was invented by 1711. Its action was sluggish and the tone thin and feeble (1) key; (2) intermediate lever; (3) escapement; (4) hammer; (5) damper; (6) silk hammer support

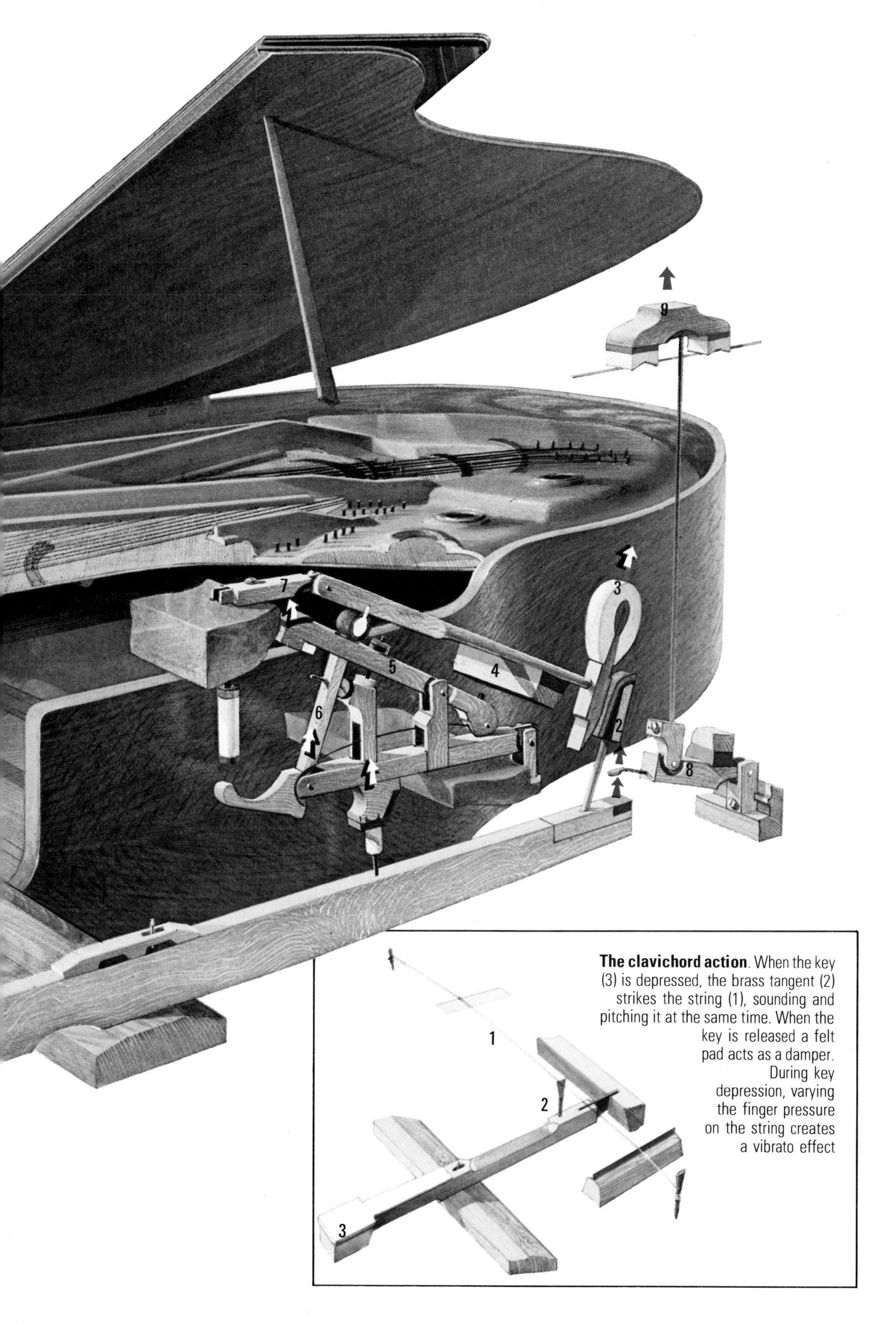

The clavichord action. When the key (3) is depressed, the brass tangent (2) strikes the string (1), sounding and pitching it at the same time. When the key is released a felt pad acts as a damper. During key depression, varying the finger pressure on the string creates a vibrato effect

PARTHENIA

or

THE MAYDENHEAD

of the first musicke that

euer was printed for the VIRGINALLS.

COMPOSED

By three famous Masters: William Byrd, Dr: John Bull, & Orlando Gibbons,

Gentilmen of his Maties: most Illustrious Chappell.

Dedicated to all the Maisters and Louers of Musick

Ingrauen

by William Hole.

for

DORETHIE EUANS.

Cum

Priuilegio.

Printed at LONDON by G: Lowe and are to be soulde
at his howse in Loathberry.

Parthenia, the first collection of English virginal music to be published. Notice the unusual hand position, in which the thumb is rarely used

The Music

The repertoire of the keyboard extends back for at least five hundred years. Instruments go back for at least two centuries before that, though manuscripts of music from earlier periods are not known to exist. Perhaps much of the music was improvised, or perhaps the instruments were used to accompany and support vocal music; at any rate, if such manuscripts were ever used (and this is long before the principle of engraving was available), they are now lost. Great schools of keyboard composition in Europe began in the sixteenth century: in England, Holland, Italy, Germany and France. Inevitably there was much cross-fertilization between them, for musicians travelled freely from court to court – more freely indeed than members of many more privileged professions.

The composers were more often than not the sole performers of their own music. They often achieved international fame as virtuosos on keyboard instruments or singing to their own accompaniment on the lute, for example. John Dowland (1563–1626) provides a well-known case in point. It must be remembered that this was largely due to the scant availability of printed music, which only began to become at all commonplace in the seventeenth century.

It is also important to bear in mind that at this period (and indeed almost up until the nineteenth century) all music performed was newly composed–it was 'modern'. This, incidentally, provides quite a clash with our own essentially historical approach to 'classical' music. With rare exceptions, when a composer ceased to be available to perform his own works, nothing more was ever heard of them. Nor could it be, since there were few copies available anywhere for distribution. In any case, it is somewhat misleading in this context to separate performance from composers, for the two were virtually synonymous: 'musician' would be a far more suitable term in a time before learning ceased to be the sole province of cloistered scholars and courtly servants, who had reasonable access to the laboriously hand-copied volumes of music and musical theory.

The training of professional musicians, however, was rigorous. A gifted child might be privileged to become attached to a royal or noble chapel, such as the Chapel Royal in England. There he would learn prick-song (a quaint term for sight-singing notated music), counterpoint and, of course, Latin.

The century that drew to its close in 1600 witnessed greater changes than Europe had experienced since it emerged from the Dark Ages. The doors of the seventeenth century opened on to a new society. The stranglehold of the Church upon music was at an end, and individual styles were free to flourish. Opera was invented, the violin was developed, magnificent keyboard instruments were built and the first orchestras were evolved. All these activities contributed towards the age of the virtuoso, and the more brilliant the performers became, the more demanding was the music written for them. This early became apparent in England, towards the end of the reign of Elizabeth I.

THE ENGLISH VIRGINALISTS

'. . . Supper being ended, the musicke bookes (according to the custome) being brought to the table, the mistress of the house presented mee with a part, earnestly requesting me to sing, but when, after many excuses, I protested unfeignedly that I could not, everie one began to wonder, yea, some whispered to others, demaunding how I was brought up. . . .'

The composer Thomas Morley, who wrote those words in his *Plaine and Easie Introduction to Practicall Musicke* (1597), shows, through the words of his hapless hero, the accepted standards of musical proficiency in the age of Elizabeth; not only vocal but instrumental as well. The composers that made this period the Golden Age of English music excelled in both spheres, but it was a relatively insignificant-seeming instrument, the virginals, that fired the imagination of William Byrd, Thomas Morley, Peter Philips, John Bull, Giles Farnaby, Orlando Gibbons and many others. Unlike 'early' music of later periods, such as that of Bach and Handel, virginal music has not seen a very widespread revival of interest in the present century; the listener would be well advised to bear in mind the words of the great William Byrd on the subject of his own music: '. . . the oftner you shall heare it, the better cause of liking you will discover.'

William Byrd, founder of the English virginal school, was one of the first composers to write songs with keyboard accompaniment

Byrd (1543–1623) led a difficult life being a Catholic in newly Protestant England, surviving a political climate that had driven many of his fellow-believers to the Continent. He lived to the age of eighty, protesting in his will his unfashionable faith, 'without which I beleeve there is noe salvacon for me'. As well as being a prolific composer, Byrd enjoyed a monopoly (together with his old friend Thomas Tallis) of printing music paper in England, and worked for most of his life at the Chapel Royal. There are well over 100 of Byrd's pieces for virginals in existence, most of which are short dance movements. Some longer sets of variations on popular songs, such as *The Carman's Whistle* or *O Mistris Myne*, display a masterly ability to develop mundane tunes and harmonies at length, with sustained interest and unflagging imagination. The very use of popular songs at this period points up an important truth: that distinctions between 'classical' and 'popular' music were non-existent, and were the products of a much later age.

Many of Byrd's shorter pieces are paired dances (pavans and galliards), the one slow and stately, the other brighter and more nimble. A great deal of them are collected in a magnificent leather-bound volume of 297 pieces by various composers, copied out in prison by a musically inclined Catholic sympathizer, Francis Tregian. One particularly delightful piece of Byrd's in the Fitzwilliam Virginal Book, as the collection is known, is a short (and technically undemanding) set of variations on *La Volta*, a popular dance of the period and a favourite of Queen Elizabeth.

Thomas Morley (1557–1603) is known primarily for his sunny canzonets and madrigals, such as 'Now is the month of Maying' and 'It was a lover and his lass'. Circumstantial evidence also points to a probable friendship with William Shakespeare. Morley has a number of pieces in the Fitzwilliam Virginal Book, which include a glittering set of variations on *Goe from my Window* as well as numerous, but less exciting, sets of paired dances. More impressive as a keyboard composer is Morley's contemporary

Queen Elizabeth I (herself an accomplished performer) dancing 'La Volta', a dance which had undertones of impropriety

Old St Paul's Cathedral, London, before the Great Fire in 1666. Thomas Morley was once organist here

John Bull, the first great keyboard virtuoso, emigrated to Amsterdam after the death of his patron, Queen Elizabeth I. By his influence on his friend Sweelinck, and in turn through Sweelinck's pupils, Bull founded an unbroken tradition which continued up to J. S. Bach

THE BULL BY FORCE

GOOD WILL DOTH GAYNE

IN FIELDS DOTH RAIGNE

AN AETATIS SVAE XXVI MDLXXXIX

JOHN BULL
MUS. DOCT. CANTAB.
INSTAUR. OXON. MDXCII.

from an Original Painting in the Music School Oxford. by J. W. Childe.

BUT BULL BY SKILL

Doctor Bull was admitted into the Livery of the Worshipful the Mercha Tailors Company, & the Livery hoods put upon his shoulders, but not sworn; this favor was done him for having composed the Music whi was performed at their Hall by the Gentlemen & Children of the Kings Chapel when His Majesty King James the first, Prince Hen & many Honourable Persons dined there on Thursday July 16, 1607.

See M. T. Records

Dr. Bull composed God save the King.

See Wards Professors of Gresham College, p. 205.

(and fellow-Catholic) Peter Philips (1561–1628). Philips appears to have led an interesting life, working for many years in the Low Countries, and being tried in 1593 for conspiring to assassinate Elizabeth and for burning her in effigy; he was fortunate to be released for lack of evidence against him. In the Fitzwilliam collection there are several pieces by Philips, most notably a noble and tragic *Pavana Dolorosa*, which is often to be heard at harpsichord recitals.

The greatest keyboard virtuoso and composer of the age was John Bull (*c* 1562–1628), who was also said to have worked for the Queen as a spy. Certainly after she died Bull made an abrupt but planned departure from England, and the air was thick with rumours. From Brussels, Bull claimed religious persecution as his reason for retreat, but the British representative there wrote to King James that the composer was clearly evading punishment 'for his incontinence, fornication, adultery, and other grievous crimes'. All that is clear today is that, as a composer for the virginals and organ, Bull was unsurpassed. His nearly 200 keyboard works include pieces of extraordinary contrapuntal ingenuity which make unprecedented technical demands upon the performer. *The King's Hunt* is probably the most famous and most formidable of these. Its variations depict with vivid imagery all the jingling harness, ringing hoofbeats and hunting horns attendant upon such an occasion. The piece is fiendishly hard to play, bearing out Bull's reputation as 'the Liszt of his age'.

One other figure of the period stands out, along with Byrd and Bull, as one of the most inspirational keyboard geniuses. Orlando Gibbons (1583–1625) was a late flower of the Elizabethan virginals school and, according to a contemporary source, was possessed of 'the best hand in England'. His beautiful fantazias for keyboard have a sombre beauty and musical complexity that requires careful attention from the listener (and the performer) to reveal the inner spirit of these works; Gibbons was not a composer of background music. Like Byrd, he worked at the Chapel Royal; it was in this role that he was attending King Charles I at Can-

Belonging to the post-Elizabethan generation of virginalists, **Orlando Gibbons** *(above)* aimed at expressive content in his music rather than mere technical brilliance. His use of telling chromatic phrases can be heard in his well-known pavan 'Earl of Salisbury'

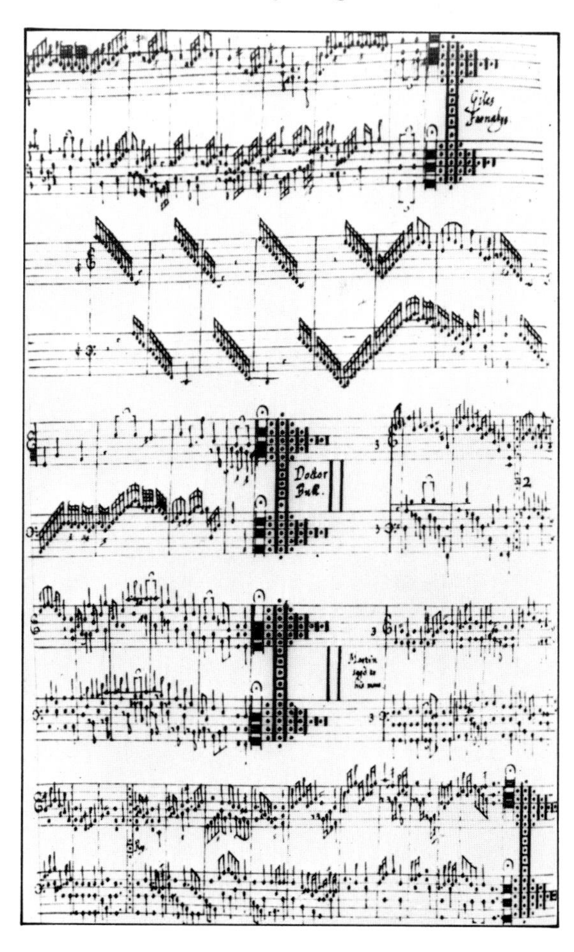

The **Fitzwilliam Virginal Book** *(right),* now in the Fitzwilliam Museum in Cambridge. The beautifully written manuscript is one of the richest sources of Elizabethan keyboard music in existence. Evidence suggests it may have been written in Holland

terbury awaiting the arrival of the royal bride from France, Henrietta Maria, when he suddenly died there of an apoplectic fit. His son appears to have inherited musical abilities, becoming organist of Westminster Abbey.

Many of the most attractive and popular pieces of Elizabethan keyboard music are the work of composers whose output (or at least, whose surviving output) for the medium is relatively small, such as Martin Peerson (*c* 1571–1650). Two short pieces by him, *The Primerose* and *The Fall of the Leafe*, are eloquent and moving miniature tone poems of spring and autumn. The great madrigalist Giles Farnaby (*c* 1565–1640) also wrote keyboard music; there are more than fifty of his pieces in the Fitzwilliam Virginal Book. Most popular of them are short musical sketches such as *Tower Hill* and *His Dreame*, which have the added charm of being technically undemanding to play. The latter piece, only twelve bars long, contains an astonishing modulation from F major to D major in its closing section.

Although **Sweelinck** rarely left Amsterdam, his fame and influence extended over the whole of Europe

Westminster Abbey, the shrine of England's royal pomp and ceremony. Among its most celebrated musicians have been Orlando Gibbons and Henry Purcell

The last of the seventeenth-century English composers was of a later date than the virginals school. Henry Purcell (1659–95) was also the greatest English composer, though on the strength of his keyboard music alone this would be a difficult claim to substantiate. Eight suites of harpsichord pieces were published after his death, together with arrangements of movements from his stage works and some other isolated dance movements. Though he worked as organist of Westminster Abbey for much of his short life, the few organ pieces that survive are fairly slight. The harpsichord music may well have been didactic in origin; quite a lot of Purcell's music has certainly remained popular in this capacity, such as the jovial prelude from the fifth suite in C major, and the beautiful and sombre Ground in E minor.

Of the countries that enjoyed a cross-fertilization with the English school of composers, the Netherlands was particularly prominent. Bull and Philips worked there, as did the great lutenist and songwriter John Dowland. The dominating figure of the period in the Low Countries was Jan Pieterszoon Sweelinck (1562–1621), organist at Amsterdam's famous Old Church for more than forty years. In his instrumental works, Sweelinck did much to lay the foundation of the north German school of organ-playing that was to find its apogee in the music of J. S. Bach. He developed many of the forms that were to become mainstays of future generations of composers, and was the teacher of two important north German organists: Scheidemann and Scheidt. Sweelinck's principal forms were the toccata, a rapid-moving, rhapsodic piece of an improvisatory character designed to show off both the performer and the instrument; the fugue, a usually monothematic piece following strict contrapuntal formulae; and the chorale variation, where a simple hymn tune becomes the basis for a series of increasingly elaborate variations. *Mein junges Leben hat ein End'* is still a favourite today, perhaps because the catchy tune of the chorale remains so readily identifiable through all the decorated variations which follow it.

Henry Purcell revived music in Britain after eleven years of neglect under Puritan rule

ITALIAN BAROQUE

Free toccatas and fantasias were nowhere more popular in the early baroque period than in Italy. Sweelinck (though he never left his homeland) exerted an influence that spread south beyond the Alps, most notably to the great Italian keyboard composer Girolamo Frescobaldi (1583–1643). Frescobaldi spent a year in the Netherlands before taking up the post of organist at St Peter's in Rome. At his debut there, a crowd of 30,000 people reputedly assembled to hear him; though the story sounds unlikely, the legend persists. The music has an austerity of style that is much admired by connoisseurs, though some listeners are discouraged by Frescobaldi's use of thematic fragments rather than melodies in his compositions. Bach was certainly an admirer: he owned a volume of organ music by the earlier master. At its best, Frescobaldi's music is concise, vigorous and suffused with rich decoration, as elegant as it is florid. A short set of variations, *La Frescobalda*, provides an outstandingly lovely example. His numerous toccatas, partitas and ricercare (a form of fugue) are always possessed of a strong musical personality and a profound structural logic. The German composer Froberger was greatly influenced by Frescobaldi, and was his pupil for four years. Fernando Germani and Gustav Leonhardt are, in our own time, persuasive champions of this 'musician's musician'.

Only one other composer before the arrival of the great Domenico Scarlatti is at all known today. Bernardo Pasquini (1637–1710) was organist of the church of Santa Maria Maggiore in Rome. His harpsichord music, lively and graceful, was sufficiently popular for volumes of it to be published both in England and the Netherlands during his lifetime. One toccata, based on the call of the cuckoo, is a particularly witty and inventive treatment of an all-too-familiar theme. Quite a number of short organ pieces have also been recorded: they combine thorough musicianship with a melodic freshness that is as disarming as it is distinctive.

St Peter's, Rome. Frescobaldi was one of the few of its musicians best remembered by his keyboard compositions

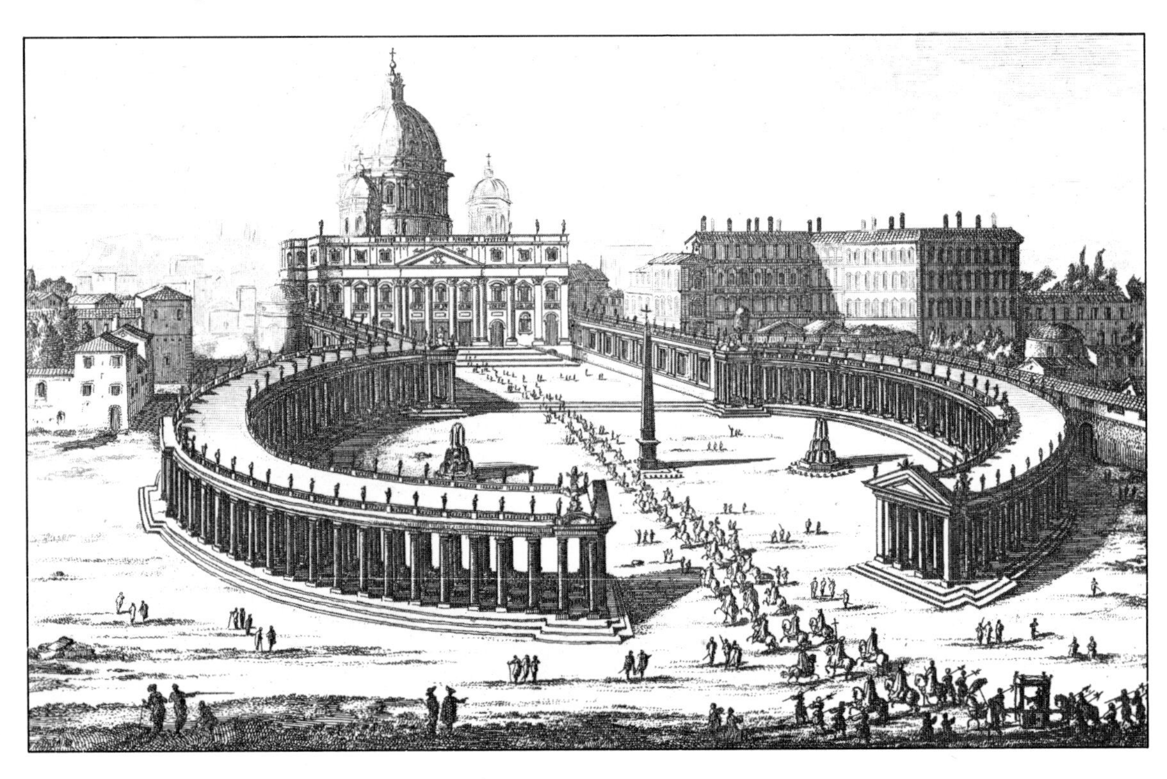

THE EARLY GERMAN SCHOOL

The north German school of composers forms the clearest link between the earlier English school and J. S. Bach. The first of them, Samuel Scheidt (1587–1654), was a contemporary of Frescobaldi and a pupil of Sweelinck in Amsterdam. Thanks to an inspired school of organ-builders in the northern lowlands of Europe, a tradition of organ-playing and composition had developed there. Though Scheidt's own compositions are not particularly memorable, his work is important for two reasons. He was the first significant composer to explore the potential of organ pedals, which more than anything else at this period distinguishes organ music from that conceived for the harpsichord. His other major contribution is his treatment (in both keyboard and organ music) of the chorale, the simple Lutheran hymn tunes that were to prove such an inspiration to J. S. Bach.

Bach was to find further inspiration in the works of Dietrich Buxtehude (1637–1707), a Danish organist who had settled in Lübeck and worked at the famous Marienkirche there. Bach made a 200-mile journey on foot to hear Buxtehude perform: in common with Handel (who, two years earlier, had made a similar approach), he was interested in Buxtehude's prestigious job. Unfortunately, the post depended on agreeing to marry the old composer's daughter – ten years older than either Bach or Handel, and no beauty to boot.

A specific influence on Bach was a volume of preludes and fugues, *Ariadne Musica*, by the German composer Johann Kaspar Ferdinand Fischer (*c* 1665–1746). This collection of pieces, in twenty of the twenty-four possible major and minor keys, provided the basis of the *Well-tempered Clavier*, a debt which Bach freely acknowledged by using Fischer's E major fugue subject as the subject for his own E major fugue in Book II of the work.

Throughout the late seventeenth century, composers in Germany such as Johann Jacob Froberger (1616–67), Johann Kerll (1627–93) and Georg Böhm (1661–1733) continued to develop the suite form, drawing upon French and Italian influences. Stricter musical forms such as the fugue and the chorale prelude were also growing in length and complexity, though frequently with a wit and charm that concealed their more academic origins. An obvious instance is the music of Johann Pachelbel (1653–1706), who worked for much of his life as organist at Nuremberg, and was a prolific composer for harpsichord and clavichord as well. His chorale variations in particular stand out from the work of his contemporaries; Pachelbel came from the south of Germany, and his music is infused with the melodious Austrian spirit.

A **plaque in Lübeck** commemorates Buxtehude; the young Bach travelled 200 miles on foot to hear him play

Johann Kuhnau (1660–1722) was something of a polymath as well as a highly original composer: he qualified as a lawyer, lectured in French, wrote elegant poetry and made translations from Hebrew, Italian and the Classics.

One set of keyboard music that he published, *Musical representations of some Bible stories* (1700), is a series of six harpsichord sonatas that are rare examples of programme music from this period. The titles are charming, such as 'Saul cured by David's music-making' or 'The grave sickness of Hezekiah and his recovery'. It was Kuhnau's death in Leipzig that made available to Bach the post at the Thomasschule there.

'Telemann', observed Handel, 'could write a motet in eight parts as easily as another could

Among **Telemann's** compositions is a harpsichord suite based on characters in Swift's *Gulliver's Travels*

write a letter.' He certainly ranks as one of the most prolific composers of all. Georg Philip Telemann (1681–1767) was essentially a church composer, immeasurably more famous in his day than J. S. Bach, and left a large body of occasional, didactic and entertaining music for seemingly every imaginable combination of instruments. But, unlike his chamber music, pieces for organ and harpsichord find their way rarely on to the concert platform. At its best, Telemann's music is worthy to stand beside that of his friend and contemporary Bach. From his study of Lully and from his admiration of the French composers, he introduced a new note of grace to German music.

THE FRENCH CLAVECINISTES

The lightness and the delicacy of ornamentation which are the dominating characteristics of early French keyboard music have their origins in the lute music of the seventeenth century. The lute was above all the courtly instrument of France, and its idiomatic and stylized mock-polyphony (known as *style brisé*) is everywhere echoed in the elegantly turned pieces of the late seventeenth and early eighteenth centuries.

The founding father of the French school of *clavecinistes* was Jacques Champion de Chambonnières (1602–*c* 1672), harpsichordist to Louis XIII and later to Louis XIV. Chambonnières wrote more than two dozen suites of dances for the harpischord, filled with lively courantes and noble pavanes. Another distinguishing feature of French keyboard music is the tendency to give whimsical titles to the pieces: *La Loureuse, La Rare* and the graceful *L'Entretien des Dieux* are three outstanding dance movements in the works of Chambonnières.

He must also have been a fine teacher: the two most significant *clavecinistes* of the next generation, Louis Couperin and Jean Henri d'Anglebert, were both his pupils. Louis Couperin (1626–61) was the uncle of the more famous François; he initiated two other important conventions of this eccentric school of composition – the *pièce croisée*, where the hands cross freely over each other in a manner requiring the use of both keyboards of the harpsichord, and the unmeasured prelude, where pieces written in long note values are given no bar lines. Such pieces are notoriously hard to interpret and require much closer attention to detail than the simple sparseness of the notes on the page would suggest. Two pieces by this young and powerful composer have remained popular with keyboard players and audiences:

The first composition which **Couperin** wrote in France was an organ sonata. Before performing it he took the precaution of claiming that it was by an Italian composer

Le Tombeau de M. Blancrocher, a short, elegiac work which includes a graphic representation of Monsieur Blancrocher tumbling downstairs to his death; and a noble Chaconne in D minor in the form of a *rondeau* – another favourite device of the *clavecinistes*.

D'Anglebert (1635–91) took over Chambonnières's job at court on his teacher's retirement. His life in society may be to an extent responsible for his numerous keyboard arrangements of airs and dances by the court favourite, Lully, which form a substantial part of his collected harpsichord works. But d'Anglebert was also a highly original composer, whose organ fugues and chaconnes for harpsichord have a grandeur and spaciousness unrivalled by any of his contemporaries.

The most famous of the *clavecinistes* is still François Couperin, known as 'le Grand' to distinguish him from his uncle Louis (whose pupil he was). Couperin published twenty-seven suites of harpsichord music, in four volumes. Sometimes the suites contain up to twenty pieces, though on the composer's own admission it is not necessary to perform a suite in its entirety. There is an immense variety in Couperin's miniature and meticulously ornamented tone poems for harpsichord, from the hypnotic susurrations of *Les Baricades mistérieuses* to the sinuous writhings of *L'Anguille*; and from the tenderness of *Le Dodo* to the mighty *Passacaille*, whose eight-bar *rondeau* theme is interspersed by episodes that build up to a tremendous climax. It is worth stressing the structural function of ornaments in this music: since the harpsichord is incapable of accenting a note by touch, or of playing a crescendo, the carefully notated trills have a melodic and harmonic purpose in lending stress where it is needed, that goes far beyond the aim of mere decoration. Couperin also wrote an invaluable treatise on the instrument, *L'Art de toucher le clavecin*, containing important guidance on performing the music of the period and even extending to directions on how to sit at a harpsichord wearing a light smile for the assembled company.

His organ music was written in his youth, while organist at the church of Saint-Gervais in Paris and before he took up an appointment as organist to Louis XIV at Versailles. His starting points were often plainsong melodies, which he combined with infectious song tunes and dance rhythms in 'Organ Masses' that would be interpolated between sections of the liturgy. The French organist Pierre Cochereau has made superb recordings of this music, while the harpsichord suites have been recorded by the Canadian virtuoso Kenneth Gilbert.

Rameau's formidable reputation as an academic and theoretician contrasts vividly with the light-hearted quality of his harpsichord suites

A younger contemporary of Couperin was the opera composer Jean-Philippe Rameau (1683–1764). His father had been an organist at Dijon, and as a young man Rameau himself held a succession of posts as a provincial organist. Often thought disdainful and aloof, he possessed a powerful intellect that would in any case have set him apart from the common man. He was a friend of Voltaire, published a progressive and controversial *Traité de l'harmonie*, and in later years carried on a spirited feud with such thinkers as Rousseau and Diderot. It is hardly surprising that his keyboard music stands out with strong originality from that of the other *clavecinistes.*

The music also requires much more of a classical virtuoso technique to perform. Pieces such as *Les Cyclopes* or the gay *rondeau* with variations, *Les Niais de Sologne*, have bass lines with wide, rapid leaps that are quite uncompromising in the demands they make upon the player. George Malcolm and Trevor Pinnock have made masterly recordings of the music of this extraordinary man.

HIGH BAROQUE

The keyboard works of J. S. Bach combine musical structure with the profoundest emotion in a way that is as masterly as it seems magical. The structure is much easier to perceive than words such as 'contrapuntal' or 'canonic' suggest. Counterpoint is the art of combining melodies so they can fit together; 'Swanee River' sounds very well when played against Dvořák's 'Humoresque', for example. Bach's unique mastery enabled him to combine two, three and even four melodies of his own devising into the most intricate web of harmonious sound; but the result never descends to the level of mere trickery, as careful listening to the bass line and the inner parts will reveal. In order to play such meticulously fitted lines of melody, a performer needs a different kind of virtuosity from that required to cope with the demonic, whirlwind passages of Liszt or Schumann: one which is ultimately more demanding in its call for perfect independence and equality between all the player's fingers.

With such an intellect, it is a comforting discovery to make that Bach was no child prodigy. When he was born, at Eisenach in Thuringia in 1685 (fifty miles from Handel's birthplace and one month later), the Bachs had been professional musicians for generations. His childhood lacks sufficient detail to throw it into sharp relief. A genteelly poor middle-class orphan (both his parents died while he was a boy), he completed his education in the prosperous north German town of Lüneburg. In 1703 he became organist in the little town of Arnstadt and while there married his first wife, his cousin Maria Barbara. Some organ compositions date from this period, which was interrupted by a protracted visit to the venerable Buxtehude in Lübeck.

Bach's next important period of employment was again as organist, this time at the court in Weimar. It lasted from 1708 to 1717, and produced the bulk of his greatest and most famous works for organ: the Toccata in D minor (with its rather weakly structured fugue), the massive C minor Passacaglia and Fugue, and the set of six Trio Sonatas. Each of these masterly three-movement sonatas contains three separate melodic strands – one for each of the player's hands, and a part for the feet. The apparent ease with which these lines interweave and echo each other is made exceptionally clear to the listener through the use of different sonorities when the pieces are played.

In the last year of his job there, when he was anxious to leave for a more important post, Bach spent a month in jail for his aggressive and insubordinate behaviour. However, at the end of 1717 (at the age of thirty-two), he took up an appointment as Kapellmeister at the court of Cöthen. The job there carried special responsibility for the court orchestra, and devotional music was not required of him. Accordingly it was here, over the next five years, that the bulk of his keyboard and chamber music was composed. This represents an enormous body of work, comprising the Brandenburg Concertos, Book I of the *Well-tempered Clavier*, six French Suites, six unaccompanied violin sonatas and another set with accompaniment, six cello suites, a collection of teaching pieces for his eldest son Wilhelm Friedemann (containing the Two-part and Three-part Inventions), and the

Lübeck, once one of northern Europe's wealthiest cities. Its Advent recitals, organized by Buxtehude, were Germany's first public concerts

Canon triplex a 6
J. S. Bach

Bach. His family gatherings often ended up with a quodlibet – a mixture of songs performed simultaneously; one occurs at the end of the Goldberg Variations

magnificent Chromatic Fantasia and Fugue.

Particularly important is the fifth Brandenburg Concerto. Scored for solo flute, violin, harpsichord and strings, the lengthy and massive harpsichord cadenza at the end of the first movement qualifies it as the first keyboard concerto ever written. After the theme has been well explored by the three soloists, towards the end of the movement it is taken up quite abruptly by the harpsichord and progressively whisked into clouds of sound; there are few more invigorating passages anywhere in music. Paradoxically, this piece sounds particularly well on the piano, the instrument for which it was definitely *not* written; but the sonority of harpsichord *v.* orchestra was then new – today, smaller orchestral forces and gentle amplification of the harpsichord can help a great deal in trying to reconstruct Bach's own conception of the sound.

As a keyboard player, Bach would have been matched in Europe only by Domenico Scarlatti. The technical problems of Brandenburg 5, as far as the harpsichordist is concerned, are enormous. Bach himself, and there is good evidence to support this, appears to have used predominantly the three middle fingers of each hand to play much of his passage-work, such as scales. There are no performers today who dare attempt such finger-work; the concept of using little fingers and thumbs only as occasional fingers proves far too restricting for those trained upon a diet of Brahms and Liszt. Though not adjudged a great composer in his lifetime, Bach was respected and even feared for his inimitable performing technique. One attempt of his to meet Handel in Halle was frustrated when he discovered his great contemporary to have already left; it is a distinct possibility that Handel, intimidated by Bach's reputation as a performer, thought discretion the better part of valour on this occasion.

Another critically important work from the years at Cöthen was the first book of the *Well-tempered Clavier*. The title needs some explanation. A hang-over from Renaissance conventions had left behind a complex and constricting system of tuning instruments that made it discordant to play in the more remote keys. C♯ was a different note from D♭ for example, though the structure of the keyboard dictates that there is only one note that must act for both. Accordingly Bach devised a system of tuning harpsichords and clavichords which compromised the tuning: the same method that domestic piano tuners use today. Everything on the keyboard becomes uniformly a fraction out of tune, and the more appalling discrepancies are thereby equalized. To promote such a system of tuning, Bach wrote a set of twenty-four preludes and fugues which would be impossible to listen to were the instrument not tuned (as has since become the rule) to 'equal temperament'. The idea was not his own; an earlier composer, J. K. F. Fischer, had proposed such a system in his *Ariadne Musica*, which Bach knew well. But never before had a group of pieces been written in every major and minor key; there are twelve different notes in the scale, each of which can have its major and minor mode – hence Bach's devising twenty-four preludes and fugues, two on each key. The cycle is often recorded (together with a companion volume – Book II, completed some twenty years later – making up the well-known 'Forty-eight'). Outstanding pieces to hear are the B♭ fugue from Book I (no. XXI) for its clear and cheerful presentation of a simple-to-follow theme, the D major fugue from Book II (no. XXIX), based entirely on two melodic fragments of four and five notes each, and the joyful – though technically demanding – C♯ major prelude and fugue from Book I (no. III).

A great misfortune was the death of Bach's wife in 1720; from this time on he grew more restless in his job at court. He married his second wife, Anna Magdalena, the following year and on the death of Kuhnau was appointed cantor of the Thomasschule in Leipzig (the board would have preferred Telemann or Graupner, but both declined the post). He took up the job in 1723, and the rest of his life was spent teaching, playing (and sometimes fighting bitterly with the authorities – school, university and civic), but most of all in a white-hot fever of compositional activity. Most of his output was of devotional music: The St Matthew and St John Passions, the great B minor Mass and about three hundred cantatas (about one-third of which are now lost). But he also published a collection of his keyboard and organ music as the *Clavierübung* (keyboard practice), which included the six Partitas, the Italian Concerto, the Goldberg Variations and several chorale preludes for organ (founded on existing hymn tunes). Also from these years come the curiously named English Suites, and more than a dozen concertos for harpsichord(s) and orchestra. Several of these are arrangements of works for other instruments, by Bach or others, notably one for four harpsichords after an original for four violins by Vivaldi. A particularly ebullient concerto for two harpsichords in C major is even for Bach outstandingly inspiriting to hear, and there is a magnificent concerto in F minor, with a sublime extended melody in the slow movement against *pizzicato* strings. (There is a superb recording of this by Edwin Fischer, who uses a piano instead of a harpsichord for the solo instrument.)

The six Partitas (*Clavierübung* part I) are probably the most popular of Bach's suites for keyboard. The suite form had grown out of the old paired dances: pavane (slow) and galliard (fast). In the hands of the north German school of composers this evolved into a suite of dances: allemande (slow), courante (fast), sarabande (slow) and gigue (fast). Bach further extended and refined the form, adding minuets, preludes and gavottes or bourrées to make thematically linked suites of up to eight movements. The first Partita (in B♭ major) is a constant and varied delight, culminating in a frisky, cross-handed gigue; while the second Partita (in C minor) takes itself much more seriously, ending with a *Capriccio* that remains the despair of performers in its fiendish complexity more than 250 years later.

The Italian Concerto is a keyboard essay in the concerto grosso form of the time, prolifically represented by such masters as Corelli and Vivaldi. In the concerto grosso, soloists are featured in opposition to the rest of the orchestra (tutti); in his Italian Concerto, Bach in the same way uses the two keyboards of the harpsichord – opposing the quieter to the louder manual – as if they were different sections of an imaginary orchestra. This is one of the very few works where the composer calls for an instrument with two manuals; the result has remained a lasting delight for players and audiences ever since.

Another work that specifies a two-keyboard instrument, the Goldberg Variations, represents the summit of his keyboard work. (More properly they should have been known as the Keyserling Variations, after the patron who commissioned them; Goldberg was a young protégé of the Count's who played them to comfort his master's insomnia.) In performance the Variations take nearly one and a half hours, and require the most consummate virtuosity on behalf of the performer. The theme is that of a highly ornamented sarabande Bach had written

several years before for Anna Magdalena; though the variations are founded not upon the melody but on the bass and supporting harmony of the theme over which the melody spins. Throughout thirty variations (each with two repeated halves), textural variety, filled with melodic interest and surprises, abounds. The overall impression made upon the listener is one of dazzling high spirits alternating with a profound and happy calm.

Much of the music of Bach's later years becomes more and more involved with the intricacies of counterpoint, as the composer continued to set himself progressively more difficult and sophisticated tasks. The *Musical Offering* (which contains an impressive six-part fugue on a theme given him by Frederick the Great) and the *Art of Fugue* both date from these Leipzig years, and show better than anything else his preoccupation with exhausting the possibilities of a single idea. The *Art of Fugue*, unfinished at Bach's death, is a series of fugues on a single subject, and probably for keyboard (though instrumentation is not specified). In Bach's hands the concepts of turning a theme

Frederick the Great playing the flute at Potsdam, accompanied by C. P. E. Bach at the harpsichord. The latter was in Frederick's employment for many years

upside down, putting it back to front or treating it as a canon against itself, produced no arid textbook sounds but vigorous and vibrant music, imbued with a spirit of the profoundest thought and humanity.

After a brief period of blindness, he died of a paralytic stroke on 28 July, 1750. Quite simply the most accomplished musician who ever lived, Bach had complete and utter control over every aspect of his art.

For the public figure that Handel was, surprisingly little information is available about his personal and private life, particularly the early years. Born at Halle in Saxony in 1685 (the same year as Bach and Domenico Scarlatti), he showed a prodigious talent, and at the age of eighteen was working in Hamburg, where his first operas were produced in 1705. His talent for opera soon attracted him to Italy. In Rome he made friends with Scarlatti; so great was the mutual esteem between the two, it is said that in later life, whenever Handel's name was mentioned, Scarlatti would cross himself reverently, and when Handel spoke of Scarlatti tears would spring to his eyes.

Handel soon made his way to London, and the quality of his operatic music quickly made him the most famous, the most revered and the most powerful composer in England; he was not yet thirty years old. He lived in England for the rest of his life; it was there that his keyboard music was composed and published.

The music presents the player with quite different problems from that of Bach. To be quite candid, much of it fails to live up to the legendary reports of his performances. Renowned for his powers of improvisation, it would seem that in many cases what was written down represents only a skeleton, an *aide-mémoire*, of the composer's original.

But there are miraculous exceptions. Eight suites, published in 1720, contain Handel's finest keyboard writing. The grand scope of the suites implies that Handel had the harpsichord rather than the clavichord in mind for performance of these, though several of the more intimate movements fit excellently on to the smaller instrument. Of the eight suites, the one in G minor (no. VII) is particularly outstanding, with a magnificent 'French overture' at the beginning and a mighty passacaglia as the close; there is no finer piece to hear or to play as an introduction to Handel's keyboard style. Of the rest of the set, the suite in E minor (no. IV) opens with a splendid fugue; the next suite (no. V in E major) contains the famous 'Harmonious Blacksmith' variations; and the sixth suite (in F♯ minor) has a uniquely grave and lyrical beauty.

A second set of eight suites was published in 1733, but without the composer's permission. These are much simpler in their approach to the keyboard; here and there they seem to call for some filling out of the inner parts where the written notes are a little scant upon the page. But there is a most affecting little suite in D minor, consisting of just the four basic movements: allemande, courante, sarabande and gigue; and another delightful suite in B♭ major. All the pieces in this collection, however, while much easier to play than those in the first set, are most elegantly turned and a delight to play and hear.

As well as scores of lesser occasional harpsichord pieces and arrangements, there are three sets of six concertos for organ and orchestra. Many of these have been played on the harpsichord; the first set (published in 1738)

(Right): **Handel** spent his early life in Italy, which explains why his music is generally lighter than Bach's. *(Far right):* The only known painting of **Domenico Scarlatti**. It was recently discovered after having been lost for generations

is specifically designated as being for organ *or* harpsichord, and pedal parts are extremely rare within any of them. Quite frequently the solo part is incomplete; in between the acts of his oratorios, Handel liked to sit down and favour the audience with a concerto, probably relying a great deal on his genius for improvisation.

The harpsichord music of Domenico Scarlatti is much harder to discuss – as well as to play. Superficially, the 550 or so keyboard pieces of his which remain today resemble each other more than a little. Some generalization is necessary to give an initial description: each of them is of less than five minutes' duration, and each is in binary form (i.e., in two halves, both repeated). It has also been asserted that the 'sonatas' are grouped in pairs, and that each piece should be considered a sonata movement rather than a complete piece, though such grouping is only occasionally followed by performers.

Exceptions are easy to find in such an enormous body of work; within such a restricted miniature form there is a quite unparalleled variety of material: Scarlatti was much more in touch with the possibilities of harpsichord sound than were either of his two German contemporaries. His melodies, he declared, were drawn from the peasants and muleteers who thronged the busy streets of Madrid; accordingly he felt perfectly free to disregard all scholarly rules of counterpoint, to draw from his instrument the passionate and glittering sounds which he heard and to transform them into harpsichord terms through his astonishing virtuosity. Scarlatti was the greatest harpsichordist who ever lived.

The most important part of his working life, the period of the harpsichord sonatas, was spent in the cultural seclusion of the Iberian Peninsula. Details of his earlier life as a composer of operas (the sphere in which his father Alessandro excelled) and church music in Naples and Rome are of lesser importance. When he was about thirty-five, Scarlatti accepted a post at the court in Lisbon and taught the harpsichord to Maria Barbara of Braganza, daughter of King João V. She became Queen of Spain; Scarlatti followed her to Madrid and remained there for the rest of his life. His fame while he was alive rested on one volume of thirty sonatas, published in London, which became instantly popular all over the musical world. For his pupil he wrote hundreds of such pieces, though the twenty or so which are familar to audiences today come mostly from the London collection mentioned above (the *Essercizi*). His sonatas are distinguished by such vivid and startling effects as lightning scales and hand-crossings, bone-crushing chords and chattering repeated notes, all built upon the most infectious rhythms and snatches of melody. It is impossible to extrapolate any particular ones for discussion here; it is far better to listen to recordings (or a concert, if possible; for much of the whirlwind virtuosity is almost as exciting to watch as to hear) in the hands of a master such as Fernando Valenti or George Malcolm.

A pupil of Scarlatti's in Spain was Antonio Soler (1729–83). In 1752 he became a monk of the order of St Jerome in the gloomy Escorial at Madrid, and remained there as organist and choirmaster for the rest of his life. Like his master, he wrote many one-movement sonatas for harpsichord. While his background does not suggest the fullness of experience which is such a part of his music, contact with Scarlatti made a powerful impression and is reflected everywhere in the shape and spirit of his keyboard works. As well as the sonatas, he left church music and organ music of great charm if not profundity. The great Colombian harpsichordist Rafael Puyana has made a particular study of Soler's keyboard music, and has recorded a powerful and thrilling anthology of the pieces – including a concerto for two organs transcribed for two harpsichords.

THE CLASSICAL ERA

The next generation of composers was much more concerned with the piano than with the organ, harpsichord or clavichord. Foremost among them were two sons of the great cantor of Leipzig: Johann Christian and Carl Philipp Emanuel Bach. C. P. E. Bach was the third child of Johann Sebastian (and the godson of Telemann, a close family friend). It was said of him that when only eleven he could play his father's music at a glance as it was being written. In 1740, at the age of twenty-six, he became harpsichordist in Frederick the Great's orchestra at Potsdam and remained at the court for nearly thirty years. In 1747, after many pressing invitations, Emanuel's father, Johann Sebastian, paid a visit to the court. The King was so anxious to see him that he broke off his music-making with the welcoming cry, 'Gentlemen, Old Bach has arrived,' and insisted on Sebastian being brought before him there and then, still in his travelling clothes.

C. P. E. Bach published a great deal of keyboard music, intense and neurotic, and stamped with a sophisticated and deeply felt musical personality. His sonatas, concertos, fantasias and rondos reject the more austere, fugal style of his father in favour of an altogether freer and more rhapsodic approach that his musical personality required. It was music much admired by Haydn and Mozart – who also owned a debt to an extremely important treatise he wrote: *The True Art of Playing the Clavier*. It was far and away the most advanced work on its subject ever produced.

In 1767, C. P. E. Bach was able to move to Hamburg and take charge of the music there, until his death in 1788. A plaintive postscript to his life is that in 1795, unaware of his death, Haydn visited Hamburg (on his way back from London to Vienna) in the hope of seeing him.

Two other of Bach's sons were prominent composers, Wilhelm Friedemann and Johann Christian. The latter, Bach's youngest son (1735–82), is particularly important. He was trained by his elder brother Carl Philipp Emanuel, from whom he received an excellent grounding in the harpsichord. It was an appointment as music teacher to the young Sophia Charlotte ('who', said Handel, 'played quite well – for a queen'), newly married to King George III, which in 1762 brought him to England and was to earn him the title of 'the London Bach'. He spent the last twenty years of his life working in the capital, and wrote a great deal of music for the theatre as well as keyboard music. The latter, though somewhat lacking in dramatic power, is delightful and urbane. It is from this very music that the child Mozart formed much of his early style when he visited London in 1764 and was befriended and given some lessons by the older man. When he died, aged forty-seven, Mozart described the event

as 'a sad day for the world of music'.

While on the subject of England, one other composer there in the mid-eighteenth century deserves mention: Thomas Arne (1710–78), the composer of 'Rule, Britannia' and countless other popular songs, published a set of eight sonatas for the harpsichord. Some of these pieces appear regularly on concert programmes and records; their melodic freshness and spontaneity still recommend them to amateurs and listeners alike.

Wilhelm Friedemann Bach (1710–84) was perhaps the most original and gifted of J. S. Bach's sons. He spent much of his life working as an organist in Germany, but hopes he cherished of moving to the court at Dresden never materialized. Embittered by the lack of acclaim which his compositions and his abilities as a performer had received, Friedemann gradually declined into a shiftless, itinerant player. Success eluded him all his life, and he was reduced to attempting to pass off his own works as those of his father in order to sell them. Of his extant compositions, most are short keyboard pieces. They are delightful, if slight, works, very popular with young students of the piano. It seems that Friedemann's genius was essentially one for improvisation; it is a tragedy that he wrote so little down.

W. F. Bach never visited England, which in the eighteenth century was a magnet for many foreign musicians. One outstanding keyboard composer who settled there was the Italian Muzio Clementi (1752–1832). He was born in Rome and died in the English country town of Evesham; in between he packed a remarkable variety of activities as virtuoso, as an eminent

William Boyce *(above)* wrote this elegant air for voice and keyboard *(below)* about London's fashionable Vauxhall Gardens, a popular musical venue of the period

Several of Bach's children were themselves renowned performers and composers. **Carl Philipp Emanuel** *(far left)*, who wrote nearly 700 compositions, declared: 'There are more essential things than counterpoint.' Bach's eldest son, **Wilhelm Friedemann** *(centre left)*, led a nomadic life and was probably an alcoholic. Despite his obvious genius, his restless personality prevented him from holding a permanent position, and he spent the last few years of his life in illness and poverty. Bach's youngest son, by his marriage to Anna Magdalena, was **Johann Christian**, 'The London Bach' *(left)*.

While he was organist at Milan Cathedral, a fondness for Italian opera led to charges of frivolity

Joseph Haydn *(above)* had the misfortune to marry a shrewish wife who used to shred his manuscripts to make hair-curlers. He spent most of his life working for Prince Nikolaus-Esterházy *(right)*, whose new palace became renowned for Haydn's music

teacher, piano manufacturer – and as a composer much admired by Beethoven. While his more than sixty piano sonatas lack, for the most part, the inspiration of Haydn's or Mozart's works in the same medium, Clementi's sonatas are important for their new, idiomatic approach to writing specifically for the piano (which had begun to take over from the harpsichord in London in the 1780s); and for their innovations in creating 'sonata form' – a structural arrangement of key and theme relationships which had a powerful influence on Beethoven's writing for the piano. Important too is his collection of piano studies: *Gradus ad Parnassum* (1817) remained a *sine qua non* for more than a century after its appearance, and remains the work for which he is best known. Mozart had nothing to say in favour of Clementi; after a contest between the two at the Viennese court in 1781, Clementi spoke highly of Mozart's musicianship, whereas the latter reported in a letter that 'he plays . . . without one pennyworth of taste or feeling'. One of Clementi's sonatas in particular, that in G minor and subtitled *Didone abbandonata*, stands out as a minor masterpiece of the age of *Sturm und Drang*.

Clementi's contemporary, Joseph Haydn (1732–1809), was the first great composer to write intrinsically for the piano, though many of his pieces can sound particularly well on one or other of the older instruments. To summarize his life here is a useful exercise for the light it throws on the position in society of musicians (even those of Haydn's stature) during the eighteenth century.

He was born in the village of Rohrau in

Austria's countryside seems to have awakened the creative spirit of many a composer. Mozart, Haydn and Beethoven lived and worked in the capital, Vienna, and Schubert found inspiration for much of his music during walking holidays in the mountains

Austria, where his father was a wheelwright. He was the second of twelve children (the sixth, his brother Michael, was also a composer). Though very poor, the Haydns were a musical family; his father sang and played the harp, and there was a great deal of music in the home. Haydn was removed to become a chorister at St Stephen's Cathedral in Vienna while still a little boy. There he spent the rest of his schooldays, until his voice broke and he found himself out of work. He moved into an attic in Vienna and continued to practise the clavier and violin. He met the successful opera composer Porpora and became his servant, in return for which he received instruction in composition. A keyboard sonata written at this time attracted the attention of one Countess Thun, who engaged Haydn as a musician in her house, and three years later, in 1758, he was appointed to the musical staff of Count Morzin. Soon the count had to disband his orchestra, but Haydn had been noticed by the immensely wealthy Prince Anton Esterházy. In 1761 he was appointed second *kapellmeister* in the prince's service, and promoted to first in 1766. He stayed in Esterházy employment for the rest of his working life.

Prince Nikolaus, who had succeeded his brother as head of the family in 1762, moved to his magnificent new palace of Esterház, which had been modelled on Versailles. Most of the composer's music was written here, in an atmosphere as happy as it was hard-working. His music became famous all over Europe, though Haydn rarely left the seclusion of his beautiful home. His manuscripts often ended with the words *Laus Deo*, as if in thanks for his contented life; the only discomfort he had to endure was a slovenly wife, from whom he eventually and most thankfully separated. In 1790 he was persuaded by the impresario Salomon to visit England, where he had become especially famous. In 1791 he conducted the first of his 'London' symphonies at the Hanover Square Rooms, seated at the piano. (Once the fashion for the piano had started, the harpsichord became obsolete with astonishing speed.) Oxford conferred upon him its Doctorate of Music, and he was received several times by the royal family.

He returned to Vienna in the summer of 1792 and later that year became the teacher of the young Beethoven, a difficult relationship that lasted only until Haydn's second visit to England in 1794. There, he conducted a second set of 'London' symphonies and was invited by King George III to spend the summer of 1795 at Windsor. He declined and returned to Vienna, taking with him 768 pages of new manuscripts – and a talking parrot.

His last years were spent in retirement in Vienna, surrounded by his friends and admirers. In 1808 he appeared at a performance of his great oratorio *The Creation*, but had to be carried out before the end. He died quietly the following year; one of his last acts, when carried to the piano, was to play his much-loved Austrian Hymn.

Of his many works for the piano, most important are the sonatas, more than fifty of them still existing in completed form, and written over a thirty-year period until the composer was into his sixties. In this sense they span the major part of Haydn's creative life (and, incidentally, the whole of Mozart's), along with the more important quartets and symphonies – which are in essence sonatas for strings and for orchestra.

In the Classical period, the word 'sonata' acquires a precise and specific meaning. It implies a formalized structure in instrumental music: as stated above, an elaborate pattern of key and theme relationships to enable a composer to 'go on' for longer, without the need for short movements and frequent breaks, as in the earlier baroque suite, or the still older paired dances. 'Sonata form' has two meanings: it applies both to the harmonic and thematic structure within the movements, and to the arrangement of the movements within the whole sonata (or symphony, string quartet, etc.). Most typically a sonata has four move-

The Esterházys' old **palace at Eisenstadt** *(above)* had its own private theatre for which Haydn composed several small-scale operas. This illustration of 1775 *(right)* shows **Haydn** conducting from the keyboard during the final scene of his opera *L'Incontro improvviso*

ments, of which the first is the most extended, perhaps with a slow introduction – as in many of Haydn's symphonies or Beethoven's *Pathétique* sonata, for example. The second movement is most often the slow one (and in a different key, to refresh the listener's ear) though it may change places with the third movement, which is a minuet (later a scherzo), designed to let some lightness and air into an experience which can easily become a little overpowering. The last movement is quick, and usually the least intense of all; it may consist of a dance-like rondo, or perhaps of a theme and variations.

The majority of Haydn's, Mozart's and Beethoven's instrumental works conform to this pattern, though in their piano sonatas the first two composers often omit the minuet, leaving just the three movements.

Haydn's piano sonatas were for a long time relegated to the role of light teaching pieces for the instrument. Even today, there is no world-class virtuoso who styles himself a Haydn specialist, though Bach, Mozart and Beethoven specialists abound. One performer who stands out is the English pianist and composer John McCabe, whose complete recording of the Haydn sonatas has led many to realize the astonishing wealth and beauty of ideas within these apparently simple works.

The cataloguing of the sonatas has been the work of a Dutch musicologist, Anthony van Hoboken; accordingly the sonatas referred to here bear a numbering system which is in general use on record sleeves and in concert programmes. The early sonatas are musically the slightest; several suggest that Haydn may have written them for his own teaching purposes during his wretched years in Vienna after leaving the cathedral school there. A more mature work, the sonata in D, Hob. 19, is deservedly popular, its quirky rhythms and gentle humour controlled by an elegant lyricism. Another, Hob. 35 in C major, has proved perennially attractive in its spry simplicity and genial good nature.

But Haydn's masterpieces in sonata form are his three last: in C major, D major and E♭ major (Hob. 50–52). They were written for Mrs Bartolozzi, a pianist who lived in London – hence the nickname of 'The English Sonata' for the first one. These works show the mature composer at his sparkling best, yet on a much more impassioned and Romantic scale than in the earlier pieces mentioned above, in particular the mighty E♭ sonata.

From this late period also dates an Andante with Variations in F minor (1793), which has a grave beauty and nostalgia that is rare in Haydn outside the late string quartets and Masses. The composer Scriabin used this work as the test piece for students wishing to join his piano class at the Moscow Conservatoire (to be played without recourse to the pedal). Haydn also wrote about a dozen keyboard concertos, only one of which – in D major – has remained in the repertoire. It is a cheerful, glittering piece, with a splendid declamatory slow movement; there is a recording of it by Wanda Landowska (who uses a harpsichord) which bears out the great critic Virgil Thomson's judgement of her musicianship: 'Landowska plays the harpsichord better than anyone else plays anything.' For organ, Haydn wrote little, though a number of pieces written for miniature mechanical organs inside costly presentation musical clocks still survive – gay music, but hardly very substantial.

The life of Mozart (1756–91) contrasts sharply with that of his great friend and contemporary Joseph Haydn. Mozart's father was a successful professional musician and violinist whose two children, Wolfgang and Marianne, showed exceptional musical gifts when scarcely out of their infancy. By the time he was four, Wolf-

(Right): The young **Mozart** with his sister Nannerl and their father Leopold

Less well known is this painting by M. B. Ollivier, showing the nine-year-old **Mozart** playing to a social gathering in the salon of the Prince de Conti

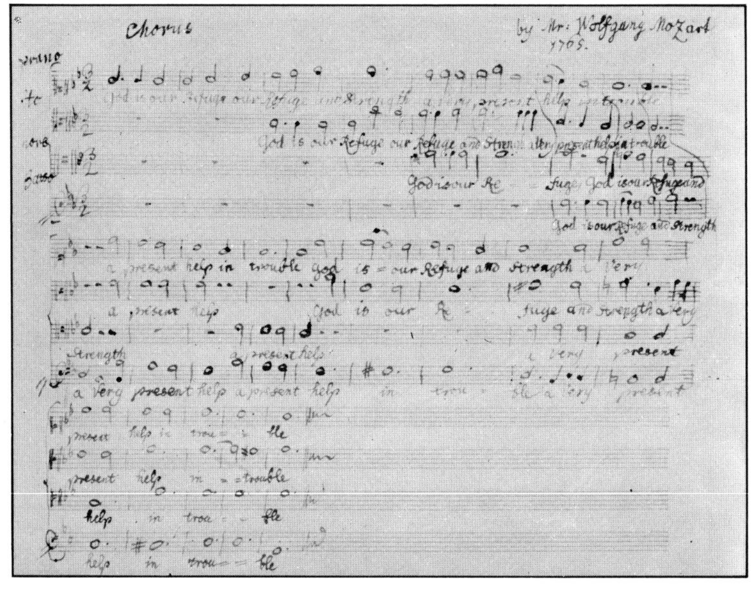

(Above): A page from **Mozart's** only composition to English words, presented to the British Museum after a visit in 1765

gang was managing to imitate the lessons he heard his sister play at the harpsichord. By 1762 the children's progress was such that their father resolved to take them on tour; their first performances in Munich and Vienna (where they played before the emperor) were a great success. There are delightful little keyboard pieces extant which were composed by the little boy at this period. The next year the pair were taken to Paris and on to London, where they arrived in 1764. Wherever they went, the family was a sensation and, visiting Holland and Switzerland on the way back, did not return to their home town of Salzburg until 1766.

All seemed set for a star-spangled future. His childhood and early youth continued to be a catalogue of successes. By the age of eighteen he had already written twenty-five symphonies and about 200 other works; before he was out of his teens, Mozart was already the greatest composer in the world. In 1777 he set off from Salzburg to Paris, with his mother, to seek his fortune. On the way they visited the famous orchestra at Mannheim, a town which Mozart was reluctant to leave, for he had fallen in love there. But Paris was not so successful now that he was no longer a precocious child and, when after a few months his beloved mother died, he returned home. His spirits were restored by a commission for an opera *(Idomeneo)* and he moved to Vienna. There began his friendship with Haydn, which lasted for the rest of his life. 'Before God,' said Haydn to Mozart's father, 'and as an honest man, I tell you that your son is the greatest composer I have ever heard, or ever heard of.' At about this time, Mozart married Constanze Weber, one of three daughters of a musical family he had known for some time. The couple were to remain poor all their married life, what income they had coming from such concerts and commissions as Wolfgang could pick up and from teaching. In 1784 Mozart was admitted as a freemason, and wrote much fine music for the order. Two years later he set da Ponte's libretto, *Le Nozze di Figaro*, a sensational choice, for the original Beaumarchais play was banned in Vienna. The opera was quickly finished and was a great success, but advanced his career no further. A performance in Prague was more fruitful, and he went there in 1787 to fulfil yet another opera commission: *Don Giovanni* was produced there in October.

By 1790 it was becoming clear that Mozart was reaching complete exhaustion, from overwork and from financial difficulties. When working, he produced compositions at a furious rate; all three of his last symphonies were completed in a period of six weeks in the summer of 1788. First performances of *Così fan tutte* were interrupted by the emperor's death, itself a final impediment to Mozart's success. That year (1790) he went again to Germany, but was too desperately worried and anxious to compose much. In 1791, he completed *Die Zauberflöte*, the opera which meant more to him than any of his other compositions. He also began the great Requiem, which was left unfinished because of his illness and death. The immediate cause was probably Bright's disease, though it would be more accurate to ascribe it to society's neglect and rejection of the composer of the most beautiful music the world has ever known.

As a pianist, Mozart was a virtuoso long before he was ten years old. Sonatas, variations, fantasias and, above all, a magnificent sequence of piano concertos proclaim him the keyboard genius of his age. The chronological arrangement of all his works was the task of an Austrian, Ludwig Köchel, hence the prefixing to his pieces of the letter K – from K.1 (a keyboard minuet) to K.626 (the unfinished Requiem).

The bulk of Mozart's music for solo piano is less egregious than the music of the concertos. Much of it was designed for teaching, through which medium it has probably acquired a lot of its popularity. The sonata in A major K.331, for instance, with its beguiling *Rondo alla Turca*, is disproportionately well known in comparison with much finer (and no less tuneful) movements in the twenty or so sonatas. The ubiquitous *Sonata Facile* K.545, overexposed in recent years thanks to the watery arrangement 'In an Eighteenth-Century Drawing Room', is still the last word in didactic elegance; its slow movement touches on an unspeakable sadness. Another finely constructed sonata of no greater difficulty and with a flowing, gentle beauty, is in B♭, K.570.

Three of the sonatas stand out as of exceptional musical importance: those in A minor, K.310; C minor, K.457; and D major, K.576. The A minor sonata was written in Paris at the time of his mother's death; it has a mood of defiant grief in the first movement, which in the finale is almost one of suppressed hysteria. The sonata in D major is the last that Mozart wrote. Known as 'The Hunt' from its horn-like opening motif, the work shows the composer's fascination with counterpoint that had come from his recent discovery of the music of Bach. The great C minor sonata is on a grander scale than any of the others, and seems possessed at times by a kind of fury; small wonder this work made such an impression on the young Beethoven. The heavenly slow movement offers a consolation which is shattered by the whirlwind terror of the finale, interrupted by ominous silences.

Mozart attached to this sonata a lengthy Fantasia, K.475, in the same key, which develops a slow, chromatic note-sequence with nervous passion and with a profound musical logic. Of his other one-movement pieces, a little Fantasia in D minor, K.397, reveals Mozart's powers of improvisation in its free association of musical ideas. A little Rondo in D major, K.485, has remained deservedly popular (and sounds particularly well on the harpsichord); but two late

A dog follows **Mozart** on his last journey. Artist unknown, this picture once belonged to Beethoven

works are particularly important, and are touched with the sadness of death which Mozart came to know so well. These are the Adagio in B minor, K.540, held by many to be the composer's greatest single work for the pianoforte, and the Rondo in A minor, K.511, whose tender grief is the more affecting for being contained within such a classic, formal framework.

Mozart had a great facility for writing variations, and there are many sets for solo piano. Typical of them is a set of twelve on the air *Ah, vous dirai-je, Maman*, better known in English as *Twinkle, twinkle, little star*. One single set of variations for piano duet (in G major, K.501) outclasses all the solo variations, however; the warmth and radiance of this work make it surprising that the piece is not better known to listeners. Mozart wrote a quantity of music in fact for the relatively neglected medium of four hands at one piano: a late duet sonata in F major, K.497, is acclaimed as one of the finest works he composed in sonata form. Two late fantasias for a mechanical organ are also often performed as piano duets or organ solos.

In his concertos, Mozart separated the piano from the orchestra in a way that was quite unprecedented, placing the soloist as it were in opposition to the orchestra, instead of making it merely the most prominent member of the ensemble. The psychological implications of this need careful thought; the soloist was generally Mozart himself – many of the concertos were written for performance at benefit concerts mounted by the impoverished composer to make some money. Incidentally, it is for exactly this reason that relatively few cadenzas exist for the concertos; Mozart tended to rely on his powers of improvisation at these moments.

Of the twenty-five concertos, several of the greatest have become popular favourites in the repertoire; some, in fact, have suffered from overexposure, a notable example being the exquisite slow movement of the C major concerto, K.467, which is now known to millions only as 'The theme from Elvira Madigan'. The whole concerto is one of Mozart's most miraculous masterpieces (there is an excellent recording of a live performance with Dinu Lipatti as soloist); in the case of a meticulously structured work like this, it is a serious distortion to present a section as a complete piece.

Of all the concertos in detail, there is no room to speak; only some outstanding stars in the constellation can be mentioned here. One of the happiest and most exhilarating of them all is K.453 in G major: the first notes of its finale – a theme and variations – were, according to legend, suggested to Mozart by a pet cagebird. The D minor concerto (K.466) is much more Romantic in flavour; it was to become a great favourite with the Romantic composers of the next century. Its elegant and wistful slow movement is echoed in another concerto suffused with the same passion (and again a favourite of the next generation of composers), that in C minor, K.491. But the last concerto, K.595 in B♭ major, is utterly different. There is a quiet joy in this sublime work, resigned yet peaceful, which, written as it was in the last year of the composer's life, reflects Mozart's acceptance of his inimitable mastery of not just the concerto form, but the entire art of music.

THE AGE OF REVOLUTION

The piano music of Beethoven (1770–1827) owes a greater debt to Haydn than to Mozart. As a youth he had studied with the former (though their lessons were mutually admitted to have been something less than an unqualified success), and had greatly impressed Mozart with his ability to improvise. Mozart may even have given Beethoven some lessons, but this is uncertain. Not long after the death of his mother in Bonn, where the family lived, the young Beethoven was befriended by the wealthy Count Waldstein, who provided assistance for a journey to Vienna in 1792 for the lessons with Haydn. Beethoven held the older man in great reverence, and dedicated to him his first three sonatas, op. 2. From then on, Vienna became his home.

Beethoven played his B♭ concerto in public in 1795 and was soon much in demand by society at salons and soirées throughout the town. Acceptance by society was of paramount importance to him. He felt compelled to behave sometimes rudely and eccentrically, for he believed that society should defer to his genius, and indeed he mixed freely and without servility in many noble households.

For early works, the three sonatas dedicated to Haydn show an astonishing originality and maturity in their thematic treatment and their idiomatic approach to piano style. The third of them, in C major, is an early reminder of the brilliant virtuosity that made his reputation as a lion among pianists in Vienna. Two years after the publication of these works, there appeared the *Pathétique* Sonata, op. 13 (1798), where, for the first time, we become aware of the invasion of Classical sensibilities by the Romantic vision.

The piano was *par excellence* the instrument of the Romantic age, and Beethoven was beginning to find the light, sweet-toned Viennese models too confining for his needs. Added to this, it was around the year 1800 that he began to get seriously worried about his increasing deafness, and to realize that it was to be more

Beethoven lavished his affection on his shiftless nephew Karl, whose guardian he became in 1815. The boy grew up neurotic and irresponsible

than just a temporary indisposition. Paradoxically, he saw this more as a social than a musical deprivation, and it gave a new purpose to his writing – to bring comfort and solace to the tormented soul. In the next couple of years more groups of sonatas appeared, including the two sonatas op. 27, each designated *quasi una fantasia*. The second of these is the all-familiar *Moonlight*, not a title given to the work by its composer. The rhapsodic character of the piece is responsible for the *quasi una fantasia* direction at the beginning, as the work moves from its adagio opening, through the sunny central movement to the urgency of the finale. The same urgency rises again in the second of three sonatas op. 31. This work (in D minor) has a sweeping first movement interrupted by the most poignant recitative. The entire sonata is one of Beethoven's most masterly and dramatic conceptions for the piano. The sonata which follows it, op. 31 no. 3 in E♭, has more melodic variety – not least in the magical opening movement – but the D minor work remains nobly apart from all the eighteen or so sonatas which he had composed up to that time.

After the op. 31 sonatas, Beethoven's writing for the piano takes on a larger scale than the works of his early life. The massive *Waldstein* sonata, op. 53 (which derives its name from his friend and patron), was written at the end of a time of great personal crisis for the composer. Desperate worries had even led him to contemplate suicide. His defeat of this period of hopelessness and despair shines out in the defiant spirit of such works as the *Waldstein* and *Appassionata* sonatas and the *Eroica* symphony. The *Waldstein* is a lengthy work, written for a piano with a wider compass than hitherto, and its possibilities seem stretched to their uttermost limits. (The work would have originally been much longer had not Beethoven discarded the original slow movement – which survives as the *Andante favori* – in favour of a short central section.) Such breadth of thought in the music requires a corresponding breadth of technique from the performer, notably in the rondo finale.

These works belong to Beethoven's 'middle' period, which also encompasses most of the symphonies, the opera *Fidelio*, and the Violin Concerto. It was a period of tremendous musical achievement. Eventually he had to give up playing in public, however; his deafness had become such that whole groups of notes would be missed out in soft passages, while those marked *fortissimo* could result in tangles of broken strings inside the instrument. In his personal life, depression and violent outbursts of rage would alternate with a rough, mawkish humour and there were frequent (though unfulfilled) attachments to beautiful and intelligent young ladies, who were often of noble birth. Their names are to be found at the head of many works he dedicated to them. Financially he was secure, though a horror of being destitute led him obsessively to hoard much of the money that came in. He rarely spent it on improving the quality of his own life, and various apartments in which he lived were notoriously ill-kept and mean, but he remained always generous to his friends.

In the same year as the *Waldstein* (1804), Beethoven composed two more sonatas: an elegant two-movement work in F major, op. 54, and the mighty *Appassionata*, op. 57. More has been written about this latter work than about any other of the composer's thirty-two sonatas. It is one of the most familiar pieces in the recital hall today, yet such is its power that it still grasps the listener afresh at each hearing. After such titanic efforts – and the process of composition never came easily to Beethoven – some years elapsed before the composer turned again to sonatas for the piano; the first result was a short work with only two movements (in F♯ major, op. 78), whose happy serenity has made it a favourite with amateurs and virtuosos alike. The same year (1809) also brought a sonata on a much grander scale, and with a 'programme'; the three movements of op. 81a *(Les Adieux)* are entitled 'Farewell', 'Absence' and 'Return'.

The last five sonatas contain the most difficult music, for the listener as well as the performer. An understanding of these final compositions requires intense concentration and sympathy. The second of them, in B♭ major, op. 106, known as the *Hammerklavier*, still sounds astonishingly modern and 'difficult' to many ears; it is certainly not music for drawing-room sensibilities, with its mighty trills, fugal passages and chords that threaten to rip the very strings from the instrument. The sonata in E major, op. 109, is the complete antithesis. There is no sweeter divinity in all Beethoven's music than is contained in this work; the theme and variations which conclude it are of an incomparable beauty. At the time of its composition, Beethoven had been totally deaf for more than a decade, to the point that conversations with him were carried out in a series of little books, to which he would shout a reply or occasionally answer in writing.

The same intimacy fills the penultimate sonata, op. 110 in A♭ major. Like the explosive *Hammerklavier*, it too has a fugal ending, but how different is its intellectual serenity from the angry ferment of its companion. As both these works end fugally, so do op. 109 and the last sonata, op. 111 in C minor, conclude with variations. The first of the two movements that make up the last sonata begins with a slow introduction, followed by a C minor allegro whose power and effect upon the listener words are quite inadequate to describe. 'He who fully understands my music', declared Beethoven, 'must thereby go free of all the troubles of this life'; nowhere is the truth of such a statement more evident than in the concluding Arietta and variations of this, the greatest of Beethoven's works for the piano.

Outside the sonatas, Beethoven wrote many sets of variations for the piano, outstanding among which are the Diabelli Variations, op. 120. The music publisher Anton Diabelli had asked for one variation from each of thirty-three composers on a nugatory waltz he had composed; Beethoven responded with thirty-three variations, making the most lengthy keyboard work since Bach's Goldberg Variations.

Many of the other sets of variations are unashamedly light music, such as the variations on 'Rule, Britannia', and another set on 'God Save the King'. One set, on the *Prometheus* theme, op. 35, is a substantial and powerful work; it has been magnificently recorded by Alfred Brendel.

Among the five piano concertos are some of the best-selling classical recordings of all time. This may be due to their symphonic conception; they give the orchestra a much greater role than in the concertos of Mozart, for example. The second concerto, in B♭ major (chronologically the first) is more lightweight than the splendid C major concerto (the second to be composed, though it is known as no. 1), which boasts a magnificent extended cadenza to the first movement that recalls how Beethoven could enrapture audiences with his improvisations. The third concerto, in C minor, is immediately identifiable as a much sterner work, at the same time freer and more Romantic in spirit than the earlier two.

For such an exquisitely structured work as the G major concerto, no. 4, it is surprisingly radical in its breaks with musical tradition: the piano enters alone at the very beginning of the work and the second and third movements (as in the fifth and final concerto) are played without a break. It is the majesty of the last concerto, in E♭, that has earned it the nickname of *Emperor;* it remains one of the noblest and best-loved pieces that Beethoven ever wrote. In the work, it is noteworthy that the composer does away with the accepted convention of an improvised cadenza; its omission is expressly specified in the score.

The last of the 'classical' composers was Franz Schubert (1797–1828). Like Bach before him, Schubert never achieved international fame during his lifetime: his reputation was confined to a circle of admirers in the city where he was born, lived and died – Vienna. Musical life there was dominated during Schubert's lifetime by the presence of Beethoven, and for years after his death much of his music lay forgotten.

After attempting dutifully to assist his father in his schoolmastering duties, at the age of twenty-one he decided to devote his life entirely to music. Ten years later he would be dead. But he composed incessantly: it is said that he once wrote nine songs in a single day.

His death (from typhoid fever) was the more untimely, for it seems he would soon have begun to make a name for himself. He appears not to have been especially dissatisfied with his impoverished, Bohemian way of life. In his relationship with the piano, though he idolized Beethoven, the sonority of his music for the most part has much more in common with that of Mozart, Haydn and Clementi. He preferred the gentle, sweet tones of the lighter Viennese instruments, eschewing what he called 'the accursed banging of even the most distinguished pianists, which can please neither the ear nor the senses'. It is perhaps for this reason that Schubert never wrote a piano concerto: the orchestra in his time had swollen to a proportion that would not easily have accommodated a soloist of such diffident sonority. Neither was he a virtuoso in the nineteenth-century sense: the virtuosity needed to cope with the bulk of his works for the instrument is more akin to that needed for Mozart's piano music.

He wrote an immense quantity of music for the instrument. Much of it falls outside the scope of this essay: i.e., the accompaniments to more than 600 songs. Instead of being relegated to a supporting role, in Schubert's *Lieder* the voice and the instrument are, as it were, partners. Of the music for piano solo, there exist

Franz Schubert (bespectacled) with his friends Johann Jenger and Josef Hüttenbrenner. The latter frequently acted as Schubert's unofficial concert agent

about twenty sonatas, as well as Impromptus, Moments Musicaux and an innumerable number of occasional dances for the instrument. Schubert's works have been assembled in proper order by the musicologist Otto Deutsch, which explains the letter D used in the music's reference numbers.

An early sonata (1819) in A major, D.664, is almost a miniature song cycle without words: its melodies are all so happily tuneful. A more powerful sonata, in that it fuses Schubert's heavenly melodic gift with a sense of high drama, is that in A minor, D.845. The tensions of the first movement must derive from the masterly use of only two short basic motifs to construct a substantial piece that is as arresting as it is lyrical: it is followed by a sublime set of variations on an ingenuous little C major theme, a scherzo, and a taut, passionate finale reminiscent of the last movement of Mozart's sonata in the same key, K.310. His last three sonatas (in C minor, D.958; A major, D.959; and B♭ major, D.960) were written in the last year of his life, and are conceded to be the greatest of the set. Of these, the last sonata must take pride of place. The serenity of its slow and profound opening movement is interrupted only by sinister trills deep in the bass of the piano: then reversing this process Schubert puts next a tragic slow movement relieved by a central section of heart-warming melodic beauty. There follows the sunniest of scherzos and again a passionate and ominous finale, whose pauses echo the disturbance of the trills in the opening movement; the entire movement has much in common with the finale of Haydn's last sonata.

The two sets of impromptus are too well known to need discussion here. Their combination of ineffable melody with only moderate technical demands has long established them as firm favourites with pianists of all persuasions and of every standard. There is also an extremely large body of music for piano duet, ranging from the gay Marches Militaires to the F minor Fantasy, D.940, one of the greatest opuscules in the literature of the instrument.

THE ROMANTIC SPIRIT

It is customary at about this point in music history to make a rather abrupt switch, and begin to discuss musical matters from the Romantic standpoint. Unfortunately, the tangled aesthetic web is too sticky to be clearly rearranged in such a brief survey of its keyboard literature. While there is a large gap between what music lovers think of as 'the Mozart sound' and 'the Liszt sound', the transitional period between them is as short as forty years. Beethoven and Schubert were both Romantic composers, though Beethoven discovered Romanticism rather too late in life to make the necessary switch. He still thought himself the apotheosis of the great Classical tradition – and he was probably right. Schubert is much closer to the Romantic spirit. This is particularly true, of course, with regard to his word settings: the *Lied* was one of the most important musical forms to the Romantic composers, who were as much inspired by literature as by their musical heritage.

The last few years of **Robert Schumann's** life were clouded by increasingly frequent bouts of insanity

Chocolate-box views of **Chopin** portray him as dying in neglect and poverty; in fact he was a thorough professional who could afford a private carriage

Robert Schumann (1810–56) was a profoundly literary man as well as a musician. His father was a writer and publisher who encouraged his interest in poetry and music. While a law student in Leipzig he began to study the piano with the great teacher Friedrich Wieck, with every intention of becoming a virtuoso. Wieck had already turned his own daughter Clara into a virtuoso by the time she was eleven years old. By the time she was fifteen Schumann had fallen in love with her. But Wieck had no intention of permitting his daughter's career to be thrown away, especially on such an indolent 'aesthete' as he was coming to believe Schumann to be. Schumann abandoned the idea of a performing career: an unexplained hand injury he sustained (supposedly through over-practising) had put a stop to that. He was instead finding reasonable success as a composer of piano music and as a musical journalist (a job for which his imaginative intellect suited him admirably).

It was perhaps his hand injury that resulted in his piano music lying much less easily under the fingers than that of Chopin, say, or Mendelssohn. Most popular with pianists and with audiences (apart from the magnificent Concerto, op. 54) are sets of linked miniature pieces such as the *Scenes from Childhood*, op. 15, *Papillons*, op. 2, and *Carnaval*, op. 9. Pieces of music were beginning to acquire extra-musical, programmatic titles, such as the lovely *'In der Nacht'* from the *Fantasiestücke*, op. 12, or less specifically evocative, *'Warum?'* ('Why?'), from the same collection, for example.

Another important feature of Romantic piano music was the free fantasia, though the one work to which Schumann gave the title Fantasy (in C major, op. 17) is really a three-movement sonata with the slow movement as the finale. It was dedicated to Liszt, and is probably the greatest of his piano works, moving from the passion of its opening movement to a joyous and exhilarating central march and thence to the slow sublime arpeggios of the work's conclusion. Even by comparison with Schumann's other piano music, the Fantasy is exceptionally difficult to perform. Less so are two beautiful works specifically labelled sonatas by their composer: that in F♯ minor (op. 11) and in G minor (op. 22).

Schumann frequently recognized two sepa-

NORMAN
PRICE

The playing of **Chopin** *(above)* contrasted violently with **Liszt's**, satirized in this cartoon 'wrecking his piano, not needing the sword he had recently been awarded'

rate forces in his piano writing: a red-blooded, outgoing style that he dubbed Florestan, and a more dreamy, reflective spirit – Eusebius. They appear in such delightful works as the brilliant *Carnival Jest from Vienna* (*Faschingsschwank aus Wien*, op. 26), another set of linked pieces. But of all these fantastic, composite programme works, the finest must be *Kreisleriana*, op. 16. The literary theme of the work derives from the exotic tales of the novelist E. T. A. Hoffmann (from Offenbach's opera) and, while the movements have no specific titles, they evoke marvellously a magic world of what a later generation was to know as Faerie.

For its complex intellectual quality as well as its technical difficulties, the music of Schumann might have suffered a period of dwindling popularity after the composer's tragically early death had it not been for his wife, Clara. She became one of the greatest virtuosos of the century, and devoted much of her life to promoting Schumann's music, surviving him by forty years. The work of Frédéric Chopin (1810–49) needed no such apologist.

He was born in Warsaw and received his musical education there. A Polonaise he wrote when he was only eight years old was published in Poland. Haydn's famous remark about composing: 'I lived on my own, and was forced to become original,' is almost as applicable to Chopin, whose unique piano style is almost without precedent. (There is a certain indebtedness to Beethoven's contemporary, Hummel, whom he had met in Warsaw in 1828 and whose influence may be detected in some early works, but this is really all.)

In 1831 he moved to Paris, where he was rapidly taken up by society, and made a good living as a fashionable piano teacher, though he never enjoyed the ordeal of giving concerts. Before giving a concert, incidentally, Chopin did not practise his own pieces that he was about to play, but would shut himself up for hours and play instead the music of Bach. In 1836 Liszt introduced him to the novelist George Sand, and their acquaintance soon developed into a notorious love affair. To escape from the not altogether altruistic attentions of their friends in Paris, the pair spent the winter of 1838–39 on the island of Majorca. In the incessant rainy weather, Chopin's lungs became inflamed: he was ill throughout the whole venture, but completed the set of twenty-four preludes, op. 28. The 'Raindrop' prelude (no. 15 of the set) reputedly depicts the rain drumming on the roof beneath which they lived. After this expedition, the couple stayed together about nine years, mostly in Paris. Eventually the consumption which had become so much part of his life reached an advanced stage, and in 1849 he died at his apartment in Paris, the man whom Anton Rubinstein so aptly called 'The soul of the piano'.

All the music Chopin ever wrote includes a

pianoforte part, and practically his entire output is for piano solo. Much of it is extremely well known: in fact there are more 'piano favourites' in his work than in that of any other composer. But the most popular is not necessarily the finest. The eccentric Irish composer John Field (from whom Chopin derived the Nocturne as a form) referred to Chopin's music as 'the talent of the sick-room', a mindless enough impertinence. Numerous mazurkas, waltzes and nocturnes are beyond question overrefined and sentimental – the more so when performed in that peculiarly emasculate and neurasthenic fashion beloved by musical adolescents of all ages. But there is a strength underpinning his best music that cannot be destroyed by even the most boneless and weak-minded performance. Partly it is that of the powerful folk music of his native country, but more importantly it lies in his masterly harmonic accomplishment, shown from as early as the delightful variations for piano and orchestra on Mozart's *Là ci darem*, op. 2, through to the last mazurkas.

Unlike the other Romantic composers, Chopin eschewed programmatic titles for his pieces, though it is arguable whether in his case the very term 'waltz' is not to a degree programmatic, since the pieces are certainly not intended (or suitable) for dancing. He also wrote three magnificent piano sonatas in C minor, op. 4; in B♭ minor, op. 35; and in B minor, op. 58. The first sonata is rarely played and remains little known. It is nevertheless, fine music – particularly the unusual slow movement in $\frac{5}{4}$ time. The second sonata (with the Funeral March) is generally held to be Chopin's greatest extended composition, while the B minor work is more elusive for the listener, being structurally less clear. There is a particularly fine recording of this last piece by Dinu Lipatti.

It is often considered that Chopin's two sets of studies, opp. 10 and 25, are the greatest expression of his complete understanding of the piano. Their exploration of new keyboard sonorities in terms of virtuosity, always with an unfailing melodic sense (the 'Butterfly' study, op. 25, no. 9, for example), confirm their place as one of the most indispensable parts of the piano's literature.

The quantity of music seems inexhaustible: waltzes, preludes, nocturnes, polonaises and, particularly, four lengthy Ballades (in G minor, F, A♭ and F minor). The last and greatest of these has been magnificently recorded by Horowitz. Two late pieces that are sometimes overlooked in the general listener's coverage of Chopin must also be mentioned: the Berceuse, with its delicate and affecting weave of ornaments over the simplest of basses; and the lyrical Barcarolle, whose captivating left hand is set against the most sophisticated harmonies.

A gentler talent than that of Chopin is in the works of Felix Mendelssohn (1809–47). His genius revealed itself very early: he was in fact a child prodigy of the stature of Mozart, though his individual style failed to mature as gloriously as that of the earlier composer. Whereas Mozart's music was heightened by his discovery of the works of Bach, Mendelssohn tended to be overwhelmed by it, and devoted too much of his short life to rather facile oratorio.

With regard to his keyboard works, Bach's influence upon him is best seen in six preludes and fugues, op. 35, which are rewarding both to hear and to play – in particular the first one of the set (in E minor), which ends with a chorale. But much of his music seems to be suited to the salon rather than the concert hall, the famous Songs Without Words are an obvious instance. Though the pieces are small, there are jewels within the set: 'The Bee's Wedding', for example, or the delightful Spring Song. There are moments of profundity too, notably a beautiful *Volktanz* in A minor.

Perhaps his greatest work for piano is the *Variations sérieuses*, op. 54. This lovely piece is a model of form, elegant melody and harmonic imagination: it should be in the record library of everyone who enjoys listening to keyboard music, and has long been a favourite work in the repertory of pianists. Anecdotes of Mendelssohn's virtuosity and his abilities to thrill an audience abound. A well-known piece, the *Andante and Rondo Capriccioso*, op. 14, gives a good idea of what his virtuosity must have been like. He used to hold audiences spellbound as well when playing the first of his two piano concertos (in G minor, op. 25). This, and the companion work in D minor, op. 40, are extremely lyrical in sentiment, very like the magnificent Violin Concerto that he wrote.

Organists are extremely fond of six sonatas he wrote for the instrument, though as far as the listener is concerned, the works appear at times sapped of their strength by being somewhat overlong. Bach's influence is again apparent in three preludes and fugues for organ, but not to artistically constructive effect. The counterpoint is masterly, but scarcely arresting: the resulting music has all the excitement of a well-assembled textbook.

The dominating keyboard genius of the nineteenth century was Franz Liszt (1811–86). Like Paganini on the violin, he was the archetypal superstar of his age, and a very long age it was: as a boy he had been kissed by Beethoven, and he died just before the dawn of gramophone recording. His genius for showmanship no less than his inimitable musical gifts brought him more fame and fortune than perhaps any other musical figure of the time.

On paper, Liszt must be one of the most prolific composers of all time, but in fact much of his published music consists of transcriptions, ranging from the literal (arrangements of Bach organ fugues, for example) to free fantasias on various themes, like the stunning *Don Giovanni* fantasia, or the famous Hungarian Rhapsodies (for the most part, compilations and thrilling keyboard arrangements of Hungarian folk melodies). Oddly enough, some of the latter pieces have become best known through being transcribed for orchestra, no. 2 of the set being far and away the most popular.

Of his original compositions, the early set of twelve Transcendental Studies is an amazing *tour de force*. They reflect very much the influence of Paganini, but with an extraordinary feeling for the possibilities of piano technique. *Feux follets* is probably the most familiar of these, and the hypnotic *Wilde Jagd* the least played, on account of its formidable difficulty. A series of four books of pieces, *Années de pèlerinage*, spans most of Liszt's working life. The pieces in it could be said to represent the very essence of the Romantic spirit: three 'Sonnets of Petrarch' from the collection have beautiful, shifting tone colours, while the late *Jeux d'eau à la Villa d'Este* is characterized by some extraordinary futuristic features. In his late years, much of Liszt's music takes on a mystical quality that is hard to describe. *St Francis walking on the Waters* is a case in point of music that was to have a profound influence on composers who came after him: Debussy, Scriabin and even Stravinsky, for example.

But it must be admitted that much of his music is display material, or frankly sentimental, such as the *Liebesträume* or some of the Hungarian Rhapsodies. Yet not all of it is beyond the reach of the competent amateur. Six beautiful Consolations are by no means taxing, provided the performer can cope with the subtleties of pedalling required. His greatest work for piano, the Sonata in B minor (1854, dedicated to Schumann), is a titanic virtuoso work, however. Its length encompasses all kinds of elements: complex chordal writing, fugue, variation and free, rhapsodic style. All are developed with Liszt's unique knowledge of the keyboard's potential. This is an overwhelming work to hear, particularly with the added dimension of live performance.

Of two piano concertos that he wrote (in E♭ and A major), the first is the more arresting, from its dramatic opening motif right through to the headlong *accelerando* which concludes it. The opening motif is in fact reminiscent of the BACH theme of his best-known organ work. This uses the notes B♭ (B♭ in Germany is known as B), A, C and B♮ (known in Germany

as H) as the basis for a highly chromatic and histrionic fugal work. Though popular, it seems to make the point that the BACH theme, used by numerous composers, from Bach himself up to the present day, seems incapable of inspiring a masterpiece. A greater organ work is the mighty *Ad nos salutarem* (1850), based on a theme from Meyerbeer's opera *Le Prophète.* At the end of his life, Liszt wrote a rarely heard and quite extraordinary work, chiefly for organ, *Via Crucis.* This did not receive performance until 1929: its fragmented style and advanced harmony rendered it all but incomprehensible to his contemporaries. The English composer and critic Humphrey Searle has seen in this music the first hints of the Second Viennese School.

In complete contrast to the flamboyant Liszt was the diffident personality and conservative music of Johannes Brahms (1833–96). By no means all of his music can be classified as Romantic: his First Symphony, for example, has been called 'Beethoven's Tenth'.

His greatest work for the piano is thought by many to be the great *Variations and Fugue on a theme of Handel*, op. 24, which, for their mastery of the form, can be grouped with the two other variation masterpieces, Bach's *Goldberg* and Beethoven's *Diabelli* variations. Brahms's development of the theme, symphonic in texture and scope, makes a fascinating comparison

(Left): **Mendelssohn**, during his stay in Leipzig, played a prominent role in founding the Conservatoire there, and was its first Director.
(Centre page): Mendelssohn's talent as a graphic artist can be seen in his drawing of the **Leipzig Gewandhaus**, the ancient market hall which had been a concert centre since 1781.
(Below): Though gruff and socially inept, **Brahms** had a wide circle of friends, including Johann Strauss, whose music he greatly admired

with some jolly variations that Handel had himself written on the same theme, some 150 years earlier. The final fugue in particular is one of Brahms's most consistently developed single movements. There are some other sets of variations as well, for example those on themes of Schumann and Paganini (the latter being technically very demanding): but none match up to the breadth of thought and the power of the Handel set.

Brahms wrote three piano sonatas (in C, op. 1; F♯ minor, op. 2; and F minor, op. 5), all early works and, with the exception of the third, not comparing well with the music of his mature years. Some of his finest musical achievements are to be found in innumerable one-movement pieces, Intermezzos, Rhapsodies, Ballades and Capriccios that he completed at intervals throughout his life. The four Ballades are particularly rich in harmony and texture, while three Rhapsodies are powerful, majestic works requiring a corresponding technique and a relatively large hand span to play them. The Intermezzos are gentler and more lyrical, perhaps especially popular for being in general much easier to play than most of his music. Not to be overlooked are the pieces Brahms wrote for two players, at one and at two pianos. A beautiful collection of sixteen short waltzes, op. 39, is probably best known, though four books of Hungarian Dances rival them for tunefulness, and are themselves extremely popular in orchestral transcription. Another piano original (for two pianos) now known almost exclusively in its orchestral guise is the lovely set of variations on the St Antony Chorale (sometimes erroneously called the *Haydn Variations*).

Brahms's two piano concertos are among the best loved in the repertoire, especially the second, in B♭. This marvellous work is distinguished by its opening horn call and by the addition of an extra movement, a scherzo, before the central *andante.* The earlier concerto in D minor, op. 15, is more tragic in its sensibility, but resolves into a brilliant final rondo. The great Chilean pianist, Claudio Arrau, has made superb recordings of both these noble works.

Of his music for organ, most notable is the series of eleven Chorale Preludes, written at the end of his life. *O Gott, du frommer Gott* is a serious and profound piece, while others, such as *Es ist ein Ros' entsprungen*, are more light of heart, though no less heart-searching. To the general listener, they may be unfamiliar: a tragedy, since they are among the most moving short pieces Brahms ever wrote.

THE NINETEENTH CENTURY

The Romantic composers just discussed all lived in the nineteenth century. The title 'The Nineteenth Century' refers to those composers whose music cannot be said to have been dominated by the spirit of Romanticism.

The eminent English organist S. S. Wesley (1810–76), for example, was far too workmanlike to have been motivated by such theatrical feelings. He spent most of his life as a provincial cathedral organist, and wrote some lovely music for the instrument. He is more significant for the influence he was to have on English musical life for the next hundred years, though the instrumental music he left is of fine quality and gives some idea of the immense esteem in which he was held as an improviser. His Introduction and Fugue in C♯ minor, and an Andante in G show well his masterly if at times impersonal style.

A much greater composer for the organ was Wesley's contemporary, César Franck (1822–90). He is quite rightly regarded as the father of not just the great French school of organ playing and composition but of a completely new and inspired approach to the possibilities of the instrument. As such, his influence was international and enduring. Though born in Belgium, he moved as a boy to Paris with his family, where he attended the Conservatoire. There he rapidly distinguished himself as a brilliant pianist. But his modest temperament found him better suited to the organ loft rather than the showy salons of society implicit in a pianistic career: he was never a socially successful man. It was after 1858, as organist at the church of Ste Clotilde, that he began to evolve his revolutionary and highly personal style of composition. But his musical idiom found little favour, and the lack of recognition awarded to his genius was a lasting tragedy to him. The *Six pièces pour grand orgue* (opp. 16–21) date from this period, and in fact found rather more favour than many of his other compositions. They are fine works: the *Grande pièce sym-*

The cumbersome mechanics of the organ at Ste Clotilde must have influenced **Franck's** music

phonique (op. 17) has been said to anticipate the great D minor symphony, while the Prelude, Fugue and Variation (op. 18) presages the great piano work, the Prelude, Choral and Fugue. It is, however, simpler and on a smaller scale.

A later set, *Trois pièces*, also distinguished by the specification *'pour grand orgue'*, match the quality of the earlier set – in particular the *'Pièce héroïque*. Other groups of pieces without the *'grand orgue'* direction are slighter works and hardly fall into the recital category: most are didactic in function. The three organ *Chorals*, which date from Franck's last years, are his masterpieces. *Choral* may be something of a misnomer, for these are works constructed on a grand scale, especially the second, which is a passacaglia and fugue in B minor.

His music for organ is matched by some important works for the piano. The greatest of these, the Prelude, Choral and Fugue mentioned above, is the epitome of his style. Long but not prolix, again this piece is of tightly-knit construction, the movements being thematically linked: in the final section of the fugue its subject is heard in counterpoint with the Choral theme in canon, against echoes of the Prelude. Despite this seemingly academic approach, the richness of the music retains a marvellous feeling of spontaneity. The rest of the piano music, dominated by the Prelude, Aria and Finale, which is sometimes to be heard, lacks the excitement and improvisatory quality of this great piece.

One of the greatest French virtuosos of the nineteenth century was Camille Saint-Saens (1835–1921). His musical gifts showed themselves early: he was composing songs and piano pieces by the time he was six, and gave his first recital at the Salle Pleyel when he was eleven years old. He studied at the Paris Conservatoire, and then took a local post as organist. He seemed naturally to have an immense keyboard facility, which perhaps is why he devoted so little of his time to teaching: one who has such strong innate musical gifts rarely finds it easy to pass on his methods.

That he was a virtuoso of the highest order is seen in the piano writing of his five piano concertos, all of which he played himself. Probably the finest of these is the Fourth, in C minor (op. 44). It is essentially in two sections, with brilliantly ingenious interplay between piano and orchestra, and delightfully balanced between tenderness and high spirits. The earlier concerto in G Minor, op. 22 (no. 2) is yet more brilliant, most notably in its formidably difficult and exuberant finale: it is much more of a display piece, though crafted with consummate skill. The last concerto, in F major, op. 103, gives the impression of having been written in something of a hurry: though put together with all the professionalism that characterizes Saint-Saens' music, it lacks the originality of the earlier works and overcompensates with much sparkle and panache. His best-known work for keyboards and orchestra is of course the *Carnaval des animaux* (sub-titled *Grande fantaisie zoölogique*). This ingenious and merry piece for two pianos and orchestra describes in suite form some of the animals to be found in the zoo: tortoises and elephants for example – and some less likely, such as skeletons and pianists. Oddly enough, the composer refused to allow the work to be published during his lifetime: it would seem he feared a reputation for frivolity.

The composer who holds the laurel for having composed the most technically difficult piano music of the century was another infant prodigy. Mily Balakirev (1837–1910) came from a family where there was much music, and by the time he was fourteen was already working as assistant to his teacher. While still a teenager he met Glinka, the founder of the Russian

The music of **Scott Joplin** *(above)* stands midway between the exuberant show-pieces of Gottschalk and the jazz-oriented 'serious' compositions of Debussy and others. Joplin came from a family of enthusiastic amateur musicians, and was himself earning his living as a pianist by the time he was fourteen. *Maple Leaf Rag*, his second published composition, brought him fame, and he was soon billed as the 'King of Ragtime' *(below)*. His music was eventually eclipsed by the advent of Dixieland jazz, but his centenary in 1968 sparked a revival of interest in his music which was probably unmatched even during his lifetime

Balakirev *(right)* built his formidably difficult piano compositions on the folk-music of Uzbekistan, Turkmenia, Caucasia and other far-lying outposts of the Russian Empire.

Saint-Saens (seen here with the singer Kutchera) was one of the first symphonic composers to use the piano as part of the orchestral texture rather than as a solo instrument. His great *C minor Symphony*, for example, uses two pianos as well as the organ in the final movement

school of composition, which had a profound effect upon him. He became the leader of a group, the 'Mighty Handful', which included such composers as Mussorgsky, Cui and Borodin, devoted to the cause of a truly national music. Balakirev made a very fine transcription of a song by Glinka, 'The Lark', which is beautifully conceived in terms of the piano – and by no means easy to play. There is also a brilliant fantasy based on themes from Glinka's opera *A Life for the Tsar*. Before he was twenty he had given the first public performance of his Piano Concerto No. 1 (in F♯ minor, the first of two concertos which are rarely heard today), and had decided upon music as his career. He was also invited to play Beethoven's 'Emperor' concerto in front of the Tsar.

He embarked on a career of playing and teaching that was as arduous as it was ill-rewarded, and in 1868 completed the large-scale work for which he is best remembered today, the 'oriental fantasy' *Islamey*. It is this work that has given him the reputation of being a technically so formidable composer: in style it owes a great deal to Liszt (who was greatly impressed with the work), but thematically draws its inspiration from remote Russian folk tunes that were such an influence upon this single-minded and neurasthenic composer. The grand conception of the whole piece is reminiscent not so much of song as of folk-dance that gets progressively faster and faster: it remains among the most challenging *tours de force* in all piano literature.

Balakirev developed into an extremely withdrawn personality, though he continued to compose. A piano sonata (the only one he wrote) in B♭ minor is likewise an impressive and technically exacting piece – not at all in what earlier composers would have recognized as sonata form – and dates from his last years: it was completed in 1905.

The piano concertos of Peter Ilyich Tchaikovsky (1840–93) are among the best loved in the entire repertory. Tchaikovsky came to music relatively late in life: he was in his early twenties before he decided upon it as his career. He taught harmony for a time at the new Moscow Conservatoire, a poorly paid job but one which enabled him to work at composition. Quite a number of piano pieces survive from this period, but they are not among his most interesting works. After a disastrous attempt at marriage, he settled in Switzerland and Italy for a while, his fortunes having improved through an ever-widening reputation and the assistance of a wealthy patron. Eventually, affluent and famous, he settled in a small country house midway between St Petersburg and Moscow. There he composed in relative seclusion, though he entertained friends who came to see him, and particularly enjoyed playing piano duets with them. His eventual death from cholera remains something of a mystery: there appears to have been some official (and very efficient) attempt at a cover-up, in collusion with Tchaikovsky's brother, Modest.

Far and away his most popular piano work is the first piano concerto, in B♭ minor (op. 23). In its first version the piece was not a success: it was only in a heavily revised version (1889), made fifteen years later, that it attained world-wide renown. Its appeal lies not so much in thematic development as in the sheer abundance and beauty of melody that pervades the entire piece. The second concerto, in G major (op. 44), lacks the melodic inspiration of the earlier work, though the finale contains much thrilling passage-work, and is technically much more demanding. A third concerto, a one-movement work in E♭, written in the last year of the composer's life, is rarely heard.

Of his music for piano solo, the most substantial is a large sonata, in G major (op. 37). It is a weighty and relatively charmless work, predictable and uninspired. Much more attractive is a set of variations in F major, op. 19: it is much more tightly structured, and contains material that is both elegant and delightful, meriting more frequent performance than it receives.

The bulk of the music, however, seems to have been produced to order, though there are marvellous moments, notably in a set of miniatures entitled *The Seasons*. Probably the most rewarding is a collection of fifty Russian folk songs that Tchaikovsky arranged for piano duet. They show how much the national music of his country meant to the composer – a fact that is often concealed by the attention the public pays to his more romantic works.

For a period in his life, Tchaikovsky was friendly with the Norwegian pianist and composer Edvard Grieg (1843–1907). Grieg studied at the Leipzig Conservatoire, then embarked on a career as pianist at home in Norway: in his recitals he often managed to include pieces from a set of works he had had published while still a student. He was very keen to try to organize a truly national Norwegian school of composition, and to this end helped to found the Norwegian Academy of Music. His life was relatively uneventful. Most of it was spent playing and teaching, both of which he enjoyed, and also writing an immense quantity of music, particularly songs and piano pieces.

Like Tchaikovsky, Grieg is best known for one piano concerto, in A minor, op. 16. But unlike Tchaikovsky, this is the only essay he ever made in concerto form. The work seems to show the influence of Schumann, a composer Grieg much admired, and whose own concerto is in the same key. Too well known to need description here, part of the work's enormous popularity may be due to its relative lack of the technical difficulty that is such a feature of the nineteenth-century concertos.

Of his solo piano music, much of the early work again shows an obvious derivation from Schumann. The E minor sonata (op. 7), for example, is a relatively unoriginal work, though it still receives occasional performance for its ingenuous melodic appeal. It was in shorter pieces that Grieg excelled. His most famous (and most richly varied) piano works are ten books of Lyric Pieces, composed over a period of more than thirty-five years. Many of these are unashamed salon pieces ('Bon-bons stuffed with snow,' said Claude Debussy), but they have a direct and unfussy sentimental appeal that is impossible to deny.

As might be expected with such an uncomplicated musical personality as was Grieg's, the general quality of this disarming music increases in the later sets. Pieces from the first set are familiar to many from piano lessons: the music is simple, but such pieces as 'Folksong' and 'Norwegian Melody' are tuneful and appealing. The fifth set of Lyric Pieces is more substantial, however: there is one outstanding miniature, 'Shepherd Boy', that sounds almost Moorish in its melodic shape. Other pieces in this set, 'Norwegian March', 'March of the Dwarves' and 'Bell Ringing' are conceived almost orchestrally: in fact 'Wedding Day at Troldhaugen', from Book Eight, is extremely popular in an orchestral arrangement.

Like the music of his Russian contemporary Scriabin, the piano compositions of Gabriel Fauré (1845–1924) are much underrated, particularly in Britain. Born in Pamiers, France, his musical talent was apparent by the age of eight, and his father eventually agreed to send him to Paris, where he studied under his revered master, Saint-Saens.

Pianistically his style was reminiscent of Chopin and Schumann in their more medita-

tive moods rather than the flashy exuberance of Liszt at his most exhibitionist. The very titles of his pieces – nocturnes, impromptus and barcarolles – reveal his preoccupation with the conveying of atmosphere and emotion. Yet, despite these influences – and Fauré was the first to give credit both to them and to his mentor, Saint-Saens – his use of harmony, subtlety of modulation and variation of the piano's infinitely flexible timbres lent his music a unique appeal. It was not, however, until he was about fifty that his imagination reached its full flowering in works like the fifth Barcarolle (in F♯ minor, op. 66). A work of some complexity, both rhythmically and harmonically, it culminates – unusually in a man of such retiring, almost diffident personality – in a passionate climax of Romantic intensity. Along with the Nocturne No. 6, op. 63, this represents Fauré at his most distinctive (and also, for the pianist, his most demanding in terms of technique and emotional maturity).

This is not to deny the value of his less forbidding works. Many of the barcarolles and impromptus (particularly the Impromptu No. 2, op. 31) are immediately appealing, both to pianist and listener: they lie as easily under the hand as they invariably charm the ear. There can be few listeners unfamilar with his disarming *Dolly Suite* for piano duet.

The keyboard music of Modest Mussorgsky (1834–81) is known for one work. Even so, *Pictures at an Exhibition* (1874) is most familiar in orchestral versions, scored by Ravel, Stokowski and numerous others. It depicts a view of ten paintings by Victor Hartmann seen at a retrospective of his works in St Petersburg in the same year that the piece was composed. The work is linked by a captivating *Promenade*, as the listener/viewer moves along from one painting to the next. The set contains astonishingly vivid portrayals, much stronger as pieces of music than Hartmann's original paintings, in fact. There is a grim and terrifying *Gnomus*; a majestic and thrilling impression of *The Great Gates of Kiev*; a whimsical *Hut on Fowl's Legs*; and an intimate picture of two Jews, *Samuel Goldenberg and Schmuyle.* Extraordinarily difficult to play (Mussorgsky was a virtuoso pianist), there is an outstanding performance of this work on

(Below): The Soviet Union's most prestigious concert platform is in the Tchaikovsky Hall of the **Moscow Conservatoire**, founded in 1863 by Nikolai Rubinstein

(Above): This dramatic painting by Repin of **Mussorgsky** in his later years must rank as one of the most profoundly evocative portraits of any musician

disc by the Russian Sviatoslav Richter.

The composer was inspired to write the piece after Hartmann's death: he had been a personal friend of the artist. Mussorgsky was incapable of producing trivia to order. His entire musical output was tragically small, limited by the onslaughts of epilepsy, alcoholism and accompanying *delirium tremens.* His hopeless and degenerate way of life forced Mussorgsky to leave many of his compositions unfinished, yet he remains the most powerful and imaginative of nineteenth-century Russian composers. A few of his other piano pieces are occasionally to be heard, notably a delightful Russian dance, *Gopak,* a miniature work charged with the infectious rhythms and melodies of Little Russia.

Nineteenth-century Romanticism led, inevitably, to rampant nationalism. The carving up of Europe after the Napoleonic Wars intensified nostalgia for a lost homeland, and its culture. Where, now, was Poland? Chopin provided the answer in glorious mazurkas and polonaises. Was Russia to remain an annexe to the West? Mussorgsky substituted gopaks for gavottes. In Spain, the same mission was undertaken later that century by Isaac Albeniz (1860–1909).

Devoted as he was to the guitar, Spain's national instrument, Albeniz's first compositions (like those of Domenico Scarlatti more than a century earlier) were a direct attempt to re-create guitar sound on the keyboard. Transferring his affections southwards Albeniz produced popular piano transcriptions of *cante hondo,* whose closest modern parallel is flamenco. The odd sonorities and rhythmic subtlety found an immediate response. Such pieces as *Seguidillas, Sevillanas* and *Cordoba* fast became part of the repertoire of all who were attracted by the 'typically Spanish' label.

But mere talent and success were not enough for him. At the age of twenty-eight he studied for a time with Liszt and, two years later, enrolled in composition classes with d'Indy and Dukas in Paris. These influences – reinforced by an abortive two-year stay in London, where he tried unsuccessfully to write operas based on Arthurian legend – finally resulted in the *magnum opus* for which he will always be remembered. Albeniz spent the last three years of his life writing *Iberia.* Each of its twelve pieces conveys the essence of a particular part of Spain, and many of the titles relate directly to his geographical inspirations: *Lavapies*, for example, is based on the popular music of a working-class area of Madrid, while in *El Puerto* he brings

(Centre page): Spain's rich musical heritage has evolved a noticeably distinctive idiom, whatever the period. The Moorish influence can be felt from the music of Scarlatti and Soler to **Albeniz** and Falla

(Left): *El Pelele* by Goya, whose paintings were an inspiration for **Granados**

together three different folk and gypsy rhythms, also used in his musical portraits of Granada, Seville and Jerez.

Iberia, the culmination of the composer's career, is not easy music for the amateur – or indeed for the professional. The variations of rhythm in the gypsy tradition between $\frac{6}{8}$ and $\frac{3}{4}$ time are difficult to make convincing, and Albeniz's embroidery of his ideas with Lisztian figurations makes them no easier. But for the listener, *Iberia* remains constantly exciting and exuberant, an impassioned reminder of what he might have accomplished had he lived longer. Albeniz died of Bright's disease at the age of only forty-nine.

Enrique Granados (1867–1916) was a fellow Catalan and, like Albeniz, a virtuoso of the highest order. He studied in Barcelona and Paris. As a pianist he gained an international reputation and, when Albeniz died in 1909, had the honour of completing his compatriot's last unfinished piano piece, *Azulejos*. Otherwise (and apart from the fact that both died at forty-nine) the two composers had little in common.

He turned his great piano work, *Goyescas*, into an opera, and it was first performed in New York. It met with little success, however, in spite of the lovely aria (from the set of piano pieces), *The Maiden and the Nightingale*. After the cool reception of the work, events took a tragic turn. Granados was invited by President Wilson to play at the White House, and accordingly delayed his return to Europe. He eventually left the United States on a ship that was sunk off the Kent coast by a German submarine. Granados himself was rescued, but, seeing his wife in difficulties in the water, attempted to save her. Both were drowned.

The suite of pieces, *Goyescas*, was inspired by the love of Goya's paintings – in particular the noisy and vigorous scenes of eighteenth-century Madrid. The pieces are Romantic in spirit: the first of them, *Los Requiebros* (Flattery), also gives an indication of the level of pianism that Granados demands. The fearsome motifs that accompany its charming melody require a meticulously trained technique. The third of the set, *El Fandango de Candil*, harks back to Scarlatti and Soler in its colourful re-creation of folk song – voice, guitar and castanets are all unmistakeably transformed into pianistic terms. The most famous piece in *Goyescas*, *'Quejos ó la Maja y el Ruiseñor'* ('The Maiden and the Nightingale'), is a rapturous fantasy that persistently repeats its luscious opening phrase, just as birdsong calls repeatedly across the night.

IMPRESSIONISM

When Erik Satie (1866–1925) died in Paris, his friends were amazed to discover – in his one-roomed flat – several hundred umbrellas. It was the final joke from a composer noted for his eccentricity.

Yet Satie's attractive jokiness does not diminish his real stature as an innovator. He wrote in a very spare style, perhaps as the result of his devotion to the quasi-Masonic, pseudo-medieval Rosicrucian order. However, his compositions resembled plainsong only in their transparency; at other levels his music was harmonically avant-garde, anti-pretentious (he once described it as *'musique d'ameublement'* – i.e. musical wallpaper) and absurd in the Dadaist sense.

His last works, the five Nocturnes, were totally serious, but it was more his distinctively clownish style that influenced composers such as Ravel, Poulenc and Milhaud. His talent is now being recognized, through the championship of the pianist Aldo Ciccolini, and a splendid album of his works, *The Velvet Gentleman*, transcribed for synthesizer.

Satie and his music were greatly admired by Claude Debussy (1862–1918). Every amateur pianist who wishes to 'impress' has been provided with two indestructible pieces, 'The Girl with the Flaxen Hair' and 'The Sunken Cathedral'. Although their technical demands are not great, these works exhibit Debussy's sound-world – one where the piano is at its least percussive.

The Great Exhibition in Paris (that introduced Gilbert to Japan, and resulted in *The Mikado*) thrilled Debussy, with its Gamelan orchestras from Indonesia and their whole-tone scales, as well as all the mysteries of Arabia. The Impressionist school of painters and poets were to find their musical representative in the composer. Throughout the piano works, certain themes are recurrent. As with many French composers, the fiery soul of Spain was never far distant. Yet it was the gentler

(Above): **Claude Debussy**, leading impressionist composer.
(Below): **Erik Satie**, a drawing by Pablo Picasso

subjects that absorbed him the more. Water as an image recurs again and again – the orchestral *La Mer* has long been a favourite – inspired by the English Channel at Eastbourne. In his piano music, however, it is not the vast canvas of the sea, but the effect of rain and gently moving water: miniatures that encapsulate perfectly his impressions. Such pieces are exactly described in their titles: *Reflets dans l'eau* (*Images*, Book I); *Poissons d'or* (*Images*, Book II); *Ondine* (*Préludes*, Book II), and *Jardins sous la pluie (Estampes)*.

The graphic titles given by Debussy direct the listener's attention to the workings of his imagination in literally scores of pieces he wrote for the instrument. In his early years, he held promise as a keyboard virtuoso, and a few pieces do little more than offer a chance for pyrotechnics: *Feux d'artifice* springs immediately to mind. But whatever the technical level of virtuosity demanded, none of Debussy's music is easy: the delicacy of touch and aural awareness demand exquisite response from the performer.

Ravel. His orchestration of Satie's three piano *Gymnopédies* brought them to a much wider audience

Like so many pre-gramophone composers, he wrote for piano duet. Earliest and most popular of works in this idiom is the *Petite Suite*, four graceful pieces: *En bateau* again reflecting his preoccupation with water, *Cortège, Menuet* (an invocation of the dances of an earlier period) and *Ballet*. Since his death, his music has retained a constant foothold in the repertoire, and has been particularly associated with the pianists Walter Gieseking and (more recently) Livia Rev.

Debussy and Maurice Ravel (1875–1937) were long considered as rivals and (according to their detractors) as imitators of each other. In fact, Ravel had something quite distinctive to offer the keyboard. Born in the French-Basque town of Ciboure, he was a relatively late developer at the keyboard, and it was not until the age of twenty-two that he enrolled at the Paris Conservatoire, becoming a pupil of Fauré.

'He was a sarcastic, argumentative and aloof young man,' said the pianist Alfred Cortot. 'He used to read Mallarmé and visit Erik Satie.' The reference to poetry provides a key to the understanding of Ravel. Like the Impressionist poets, he sought to convey reality rather than indeterminate ideas. From his first major work, *Jeux d'eau* (1901), to the song-cycle *Don Quichotte à Dulcinée* (written shortly before his death from brain tumour in 1937), most of his work attempted to capture emotions, pictures and atmosphere. The titles are significant. In *Miroirs* (1905) he depicted, one after the other: night moths, sad birds, an ocean liner and a valley full of bells (the French titles sound more poetic). The Spanish composer Manuel de Falla once said that only a Frenchman could write really Spanish music. He was probably thinking of Ravel. His first Spanish piece, *Habañera*, was later orchestrated in *Rapsodie espagnole*, and his sympathy with Iberia finally culminated in the work best known to the public – *Bolero*.

Ravel's two piano concertos date from the same year – 1931. The first, in G major, was intentionally 'light-hearted and brilliant, not aiming at profundity or effect'. He had originally intended to perform the concerto himself, but eventually passed it to Marguerite Long to play, and instead Ravel conducted. But before the G major concerto was performed, Ravel's second concerto, in D major, for the left hand alone, was given in Vienna by Paul Wittgenstein, who had lost his right arm during the First

World War. The D major concerto is a much more powerful work, its jazz elements, as much as its novelty, contributing to its popularity.

The music of Alexander Scriabin (1872–1915) has its own equally fervent proponents and detractors. In his early years, Chopin was a strong influence upon this impressionable and eccentric musician: the very titles of pieces from these years prove the point – nocturnes, studies, waltzes and mazurkas – music written with an audience in mind.

Born in Moscow, he studied at the Conservatoire there under Taneyev and Arensky, and was quickly taken under the wing of Belaiev, a timber merchant and enthusiastic musical amateur who founded a publishing firm to promote the cause of the Russian Nationalist school of composers. An accident while practising Balakirev's *Islamey* inclined him to composition: a Prelude and Nocturne (op. 9) for left hand alone presage the commissions to Ravel and others by Paul Wittgenstein, the one-armed virtuoso of the twentieth century.

Although showing signs of mental instability as a child, it was only later that Scriabin succumbed to the cult of theosophy, which he then tried to express in his music. Chord structures based on ascending fourths, distinctive melodic shapes and complex rhythms are woven into highly charged units, finely wrought to swell into monumental, and at times half-crazed, climaxes.

The sad truth was that Scriabin thought he was God. This meant that in order to convey his divine message, he had to devastate his dwindling audiences. Foreshadowing the twentieth-century enthusiasm for multi-media presentations, he added scents to the air, specifying changes to them as the works progressed. He gave to each note a colour (C was red, E pearly white and shimmer of moonlight) and lights projected them as the notes were played. He planned his final work to be performed in India, and to include architecture, sculpture, light and smell, hoping to 'suffocate in ecstasy'. Sadly, in 1915, a septic lip gave him blood poisoning, which resulted in a less spectacular death.

The ten piano sonatas run parallel with Scriabin's mental development. The first five are almost Brahmsian, though the title of no. 3, *States of Soul*, suggests that mental derangement was there in seed. The last five sonatas are firmly rooted in 'mystic harmony'. By the seventh, he was finding the limitations of the keyboard difficult to accept.

Like Debussy, Scriabin titled many of his pieces, and these display the state of his mind and of his preoccupations: *Poem of Fire, Poem of Ecstasy, The Divine Poem*, and *The Satanic Poem*, the *White Mass* Sonata (no. 7) and the *Black Mass* Sonata (no. 9).

The 1960s witnessed a revival of interest in his music, with Vladimir Ashkenazy and John Ogdon (both winners of the Tchaikovsky competition) in the vanguard.

Contemporary with Scriabin at the Moscow Conservatoire (and taught by the same masters), Sergei Rachmaninov (1873–1943) was rapidly an international success. Born in Novgorod on All Fools' Day, he displayed the not uncommon mixture of phenomenal facility and indolence, though his talent kept him apace with his fellow students. But once in Moscow, he began to apply himself to gaining the technique that was to excite audiences for the next fifty years.

His prelude in C♯ minor was performed in London when its composer was twenty, and soon Rachmaninov was known everywhere. But success did not follow quite so willingly. The happy-go-lucky young man became melancholic: the tendency stayed with him for the rest of his life. Undergoing treatment by hypnosis, he was told: 'You will write a concerto . . . the concerto will be of excellent quality.' It was. The piano concerto no. 2 in C minor, op. 18, was an immense success, and has remained one of the most popular works with pianists and audiences. Its style developed naturally from that of Tchaikovksy, offering marvellous opportunities for virtuoso display, yet inhabiting a dream-world of scented melody and histrionic emotion.

The next concerto, in D minor, op. 30, 'a fitting epilogue to the era of the Romantic piano concerto', is cast in a Lisztian mould, written to show off the composer's mastery of the keyboard as well as his mastery of form. In 1910 came the last set of Preludes (to follow two earlier sets of 1892 and 1903). These twenty-four pieces demonstrate better than anything else the development of the composer's sophistication of virtuosity and his consummate absorption of keyboard styles.

The 1917 revolution in Russia forced a major crisis on Rachmaninov. At home in Moscow he was tormented by the threat to his wife and family. He worked on his fourth piano concerto (in G minor, op. 40), though acute stress made concentration all but impossible. Deliverance came with the offer of a Scandinavian concert tour, and he secured passports for himself and

(Right): **Rachmaninov** in 1929. Innovative musical thought is not always the key to commercial success, as the 19th-century style of his second piano concerto demonstrates. *(Below):* **Scriabin** – visionary, mystic, composer of genius and virtuoso of the highest order

all his family. Concealing his real intentions, he left with one small suitcase, abandoning most of his belongings. Until 1927 he remained silent as a composer, and when the fourth concerto at last received its première, it was as though Rachmaninov could only repeat clichés from his earlier work.

The creative urge returned slowly; in 1934 Rachmaninov produced the *Rhapsody on a Theme by Paganini* (a theme that had been used before him by Brahms and Liszt). At last the virtuosity was back: from a deceptively simple opening, the work displays progressively the entire *batterie* of a nineteenth-century master of the keyboard, and has remained (with the second concerto) the public's favourite of his compositions.

After 1917, Rachmaninov made his home in the United States – and in Switzerland – and developed a strong relationship with Leopold Stokowski and the Philadelphia Orchestra. His tripartite career as pianist, composer and conductor is magnificently documented on disc: all of his major works have been recorded with himself either as maestro or soloist. He died in Beverly Hills, a twentieth-century anachronism from the late Romantic tradition.

Pianists today are more likely to curse Max Reger (1873–1916) than to praise him. His transcriptions of Bach (the Brandenburg Concertos, for example) for piano duet are so tortuous that each player seems to need several extra fingers if a performance is not to end in a fight to the death.

But Reger's life was not dependent on such bread-and-butter works. Now remembered for his championing of earlier German composers, he was much admired once for his own rather derivative *boudoir* pieces. Quite early in his career, he discarded the influence of Wagner, which had first drawn him to a life in music, against his father's wishes. Reger based his compositions upon earlier models. His piano variations on a theme of Bach, op. 81 (taken from Cantata no. 128), are well beyond the reach of the pianistic dilettante; but his shorter pieces in the vein of Schubert and Brahms (such as *Aus Meinem Tagebuch*, op. 82) have a naïve charm, and are simple enough for the less ambitious to while away a pleasant evening.

THE TWENTIETH CENTURY

A profound change, comparable with the switch from plainsong to polyphony many centuries earlier, was about to occur in Western music. There was no absolute revolution, no theses nailed to the doors of Wittenberg. Yet Ravel, 'modern' though he appeared to his contemporaries, sensed that something entirely new was in the offing, and was disgusted. 'How can you reduce music to a logical syllogism or to a mathematical formula?', he asked, '. . . music . . . must always be emotional first and intellectual second. That is why, in composing, I have never been tempted by the radical style of the young. . . .'

Arnold Schoenberg (1874–1951) was the prime culprit. He completely freed music from any responsibility of pleasing the ear in the traditional manner – though he seriously hoped his melodies would one day be whistled in the streets by errand boys: an ambition which remains unfulfilled. His early works shocked the Viennese public (though they won the admiration of both Mahler and Richard Strauss). Three Pieces, op. 11, and Six Easy Pieces, op. 19, while still nominally tonal, break away from all conventions of harmonic progression and melodic structure.

It was during a musically abstinent period of painting that Schoenberg evolved the twelve-tone system, a compositional process through which no note may be repeated until all eleven others have been sounded. In the Five Pieces, op. 23 (completed in 1923, twelve years after the last set), appears a Waltz that is entirely and strictly serial (twelve-tone). The music still shocks today, though it is meticulously and sensitively conceived in terms of the piano. The pieces are so short as to bear repeated listening. The ear accustoms readily to dissonance once the shock has worn off.

Schoenberg's two distinguished disciples wrote little for the keyboard. Alban Berg's (1885–1935) sole contribution to the repertoire being a Sonata (op. 1), a late Romantic work in classical form. Anton Webern (1883–1945) also wrote only one solo piano work, the Variations, op. 27. It was written in 1936, and the composer referred to it as 'a sort of suite'. While the score looks fairly simple, the subtlety of phrasing combined with multiple syncopations make this endearing work elusive in performance.

While the Viennese were experiencing the discipline of a new musical anarchy, a wealthy businessman, Charles Ives (1874–1954), was carrying on the good work in the United States. He combined tunes learned in his youth, brass band music and revivalist hymns, for example, with a hilarious, sentimental polytonality. His formidably difficult Concord Sonata is a typical example of his idiom. Studied simplicity is side by side with cacophony, rhythmic distortion and exuberant, devil-may-care counterpoint. In the second movement of his Sonata No. 1 he uses bar-room choruses as a linking motif. The Three-Page Sonata pokes fun at tradition with rare wit, while in a work entitled 'Some South-paw Pitching' the composer offers pertinent

For years the parlour piano was the focus of family social life. The piano stool would contain a tutor, descriptive pieces such as *The Robin's Return*, and some piano duets. There might even be a score of *Messiah*, but it is unlikely that Bach's *'48'* would find a place there. Yet in the year (1910) that this comfortable family group was photographed, **Schoenberg** *(below)* was evolving the twelve-note system which was to overthrow the musical establishment

exercise for developing left-hand dexterity.

At the same time as America was enjoying its late-found musical nationalism, a young Spanish composer, Manuel de Falla (1876–1946), was perfecting the earlier nationalist intentions of Albeniz and Granados. Born in Cadiz, he studied for a time at the Madrid Conservatoire before taking a week's holiday in Paris, where he found the company of Debussy, Ravel and Paul Dukas so stimulating that he stayed for seven years.

Four Spanish Pieces for piano (1909) were conventional in their use of native folk rhythms. It was not for another six years that, with *Nights in the Gardens of Spain* for piano and orchestra, he revealed his true originality. *Fantasia Baetica*, his only extended solo piano work, followed in 1919, but, despite the championing of Artur Rubinstein (for whom it was written), the work never achieved popular success. His Harpsichord Concerto, with its insistent drive and harsh harmonies, remains the outstanding modern work for that instrument.

One of the greatest pianist-composers of the twentieth century was Béla Bartók (1881–1945). His life was beset by bitterness and tragedy, for he was deprived of the recognition that was his due while he watched his beloved homeland being torn apart. After attending the conservatoire in Budapest, he began to compose in earnest and, with his friend Kodály, set out to explore his native folk music. Political developments that were to crush Hungary for a second time drove Bartók to the United States in 1940. There he hoped to meet with success, but it never came. He died there, of starvation and leukaemia, just as his genius was being acclaimed in his native land.

His musical idiom is readily recognizable. His taut, uncompromising harmonies, in place of the lush sounds of his popular contemporary, Rachmaninov, have tended to alienate listeners. The three piano concertos (now among the most played of twentieth-century works in this form) have a distinct menacing quality that makes many approach them only with caution.

(Top): **Bartók** in Basle, 1937, before the world première of his *Music for Strings, Percussion, and Celesta*. *(Below)*: **Prokofiev** at his country retreat in 1951

The first (written in 1926) is the most dissonant, written at the beginning of Bartók's most experimental period. Its imaginative use of percussion as part of the accompanying texture is startling. The second concerto (1932), though still in an acerbic and discordant vein, is more approachable, through the excitement of the outer movements: the magical passages of ninths in the central movement are almost an echo of Debussy. The most immediately attractive of the concertos is the third, composed in the year of his death. (It is also the easiest to play.) One more work with accompaniment, though far more demanding for players and listeners, is the Sonata for Two Pianos and Percussion. Martha Argerich and Stephen Bishop-Kovacevich have made a thrilling recording of this piece, fully exploiting its amazing range of sonorities.

Bartók's *magnum opus* for solo piano, *Mikrokosmos*, was composed over a period of eleven years. Beginning as a series of didactic pieces for his son, it finished as a set of six books, comprising no less than 153 pieces. The work becomes progressively harder. By the time of the last book, the rhythmic structure has reached virtuoso level. *Mikrokosmos* also includes the extraordinary 'Diary of a Fly', a unique work of buzzing intensity that harks back to the French keyboard tone poems of the eighteenth century.

Equally absorbed in piano sound (though less in command of its sonority) was the fanciful imagination of Igor Stravinsky (1882–1971). Accordingly, his solo piano music is small in quantity: he needed the palette of exotic orchestra and vocal sounds to express his impressive command of Asian styles, though he utilized the piano a great deal as part of the orchestra. 'Piano Rag Music' is based on the early sounds of cat-house jazz. 'Three Movements from Petroushka' was based upon his magical ballet, and arranged in 1921 for Artur Rubinstein, who had popularized the work in his own arrangement. The elegant *'Sérénade en La'* (1925), commissioned for an early 78 rpm recording, has spiritually much in common with eighteenth-century *Nachtmusik*.

Stravinsky worked for much of his life in the theatre. In this he had, surprisingly, much in common with the great organists of the twentieth century. After a thousand years, the organ remains for many the king of keyboard instruments (it was Mozart who initiated that particular cliché). Its ceremonial grandeur, and the variety of its voices, were marvellously exploited by the German virtuoso Sigfried Karg-Elert (1877–1933). Best remembered today for his brilliant chorale prelude on *Now Thank We All Our God*, he studied in Leipzig and, after establishing his reputation as a pianist, transferred his affections to the organ.

But while others disported themselves seriously at the organ, nationalism was still rife in the remoter parts of Europe. Sergei Prokofiev (1891–1955) followed Rachmaninov's example and abandoned Mother Russia, on an extended concert tour in 1918. His need to compose had resulted in numerous piano pieces and an opera by the age of nine; after formal instruction (with Glière) he produced two more operas, a violin sonata, a symphony and two piano sonatas. Enrolled in 1904 into the St Petersburg Conservatoire, he studied with Liadov, Rimsky-Korsakov and Tcherepnin. On leaving Russia (via Siberia and Japan), Prokofiev's piano-playing created a sensation in the United States. Continuing his eastward journey, he arrived in Paris, and there Diaghilev encouraged him to compose.

By 1933, he felt able to return to Russia, and died there – though he continued his concert tours in the West. His music was made up of four essential elements: formalism, that revered the structures of the eighteenth century; innovation, which motivated his compositional process in the first place; a motoric element, driving each work onwards to its conclusion; and finally a sense of lyricism: surrounded as he was by the atonal developments of his contemporaries, Prokofiev respected the public's love of a good tune.

His five piano concertos illustrate these elements well. No. 1 (in D♭ major) stresses the motoric element. In the second concerto, however, the composer is creating a virtuoso work to display all his finest pianistic qualities, and makes room for meditative phrases in contrast to the brassy glitter. The third concerto (in C major, op. 26) is probably his most important work in the medium. A wide imaginative range, with marvellously ingenious orchestration, exotic figures and brilliant keyboard style, is assembled with a sardonic wit that has kept this arresting work on the concert platform. It is rivalled for brilliance only by the fifth concerto, which demands a consummate virtuosity.

The *Visions fugitives* (op. 22) have a strong French influence, and from his operas and ballets Prokofiev later arranged several piano solos that have found their way into the popular repertoire: the march from *The Love of Three Oranges*, for example, or pieces from *Romeo and Juliet* are favourite encores in piano versions.

Dmitri Shostakovich (1906–77) was frightened, not to say terrified, by Stalin's criticism of his *'petit bourgeois'* music. He felt impelled to respond, in his Fifth Symphony, by sub-titling it 'A Soviet Artist's Reply to Just Criticism'.

Shostakovich's greatest keyboard work, the

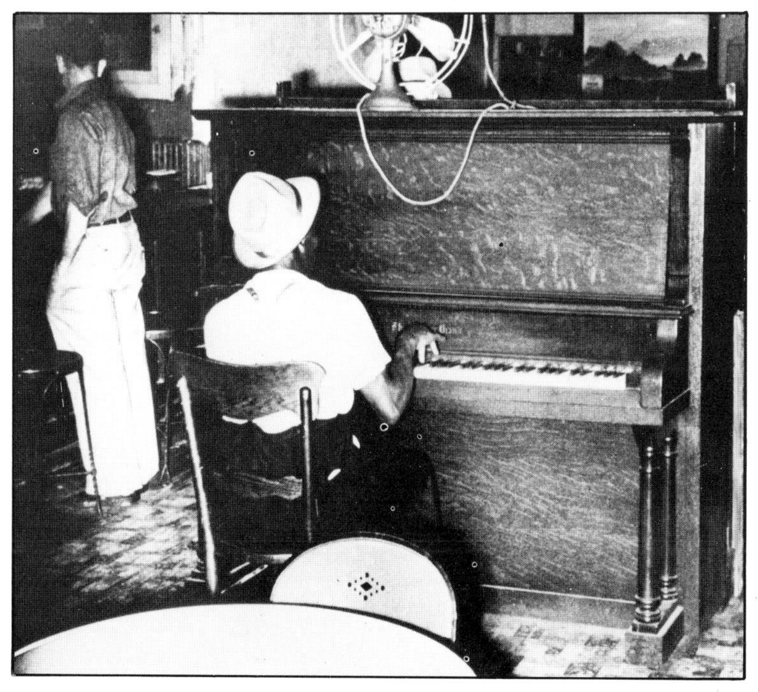

From its honky-tonk origins *(right)* jazz achieved the respectability and status of an art form when given a touch of genius by an artist such as **Duke Ellington** *(above)*

twenty-four Preludes and Fugues, op. 87, was written in celebration of the bicentenary of Bach's death. (They have little in common with an earlier set of twenty-four preludes, op. 34.) A more dissonant, stormy work is the first piano sonata, op. 12, another example of Shostakovich's tortured, highly personal style that was to prove so unacceptable in Russia.

The German Paul Hindemith (1895–1963) was also attacked for the modernism of his music and forced to flee his country. (He eventually settled in the United States as head of the Yale music department.) His early years had been spent as violinist in dance bands, cinemas and café orchestras, and his music, though eclectic and not unmodern, was powerfully formal. *Ludus Tonalis*, his keyboard masterpiece, is an uncompromising embodiment of his musical principles. Subtitled 'Studies in Counterpoint, Tonal Organization and Piano Playing', it consists of twelve fugues, interspersed with interludes and enclosed within a prelude and postlude. Its structure has strong links with some of Bach's fugal works, such as *The Art of Fugue* or *The Musical Offering*.

Hindemith's musical vitality and strong logical sense are well displayed in three piano sonatas (1936) and three sonatas for organ (the latter have been splendidly recorded by Lionel Rogg). An impressive Piano Concerto (1945) is remarkable for the originality of its orchestration, and for a brilliant last movement, entitled 'Medley'.

Francis Poulenc (1899–1963) was one of the close-knit group of composers known as *Les Six*. Though they felt themselves to be a coterie, they were never entirely clear about their corporate aims.

Poulenc early distinguished himself by the *Concert Champêtre* for harpsichord and orchestra, a work as original as Falla's though in a pastoral vein. Full of *joie de vivre*, the concerto remains popular and has been well recorded by Landowska (for whom it was written), George Malcolm and Zuzana Ruzickova.

As might be expected from a close friend of Satie, Poulenc's keyboard works were characteristically gay, witty and sometimes dismissed by the envious as 'salon' or 'Music-hall' in style. His first work, *Rapsodie nègre*, was written as a deliberate spoof when he was eighteen. It was an immediate success, and between 1918 and 1935 he produced eleven volumes of piano pieces, ranging from child's-play to the most bravura figurations. Three *Mouvements perpetuels* are probably the best known.

Poulenc's wit and economy of style extended to larger-scale works, most notably in the Concerto in D minor for two pianos and orchestra, memorably recorded by the composer in typically skittish mood. He also wrote two sonatas for two pianos, well within the range of amateurs, as is a piano duet sonata.

The explanations that Olivier Messiaen (1903 . . .) has written of the theories behind his music seem bizarre to his detractors. But the justification is in the powerful individuality and intensity of his style.

After studying at the Paris Conservatoire with Dukas and Dupré, he became organist at La Sainte-Trinité, a position he retained for more than forty years. His large corpus of works for organ was written with that church's instrument in mind. Representative of his organ style is *Méditations sur le mystère de la Sainte-Trinité*, where Messiaen ascribed pitch and length to each letter of the alphabet, applying these sounds to mystical texts for his thematic material.

Birdsong has been of great importance to the composer, and he has transformed it into many piano pieces. In *Oiseaux exotiques*, for piano and orchestra, he lists over fifty birds, indicating in the score where their calls are imitated. Another work, for solo piano, on the same idea (and in seven books) is the *Catalogue des oiseaux*. The work is dedicated to his wife, the pianist Yvonne Loriod. Other influences upon Messiaen (Indian ragas and the gamelan orchestra) are brought together in the *Turangalîla* Symphony, which is almost a piano concerto, and contains an important part for a keyboard instrument whose eerie, electronic wail has often been prominent in his music, the Ondes Martenot.

Messiaen's fascinating and complex music is readily available on disc. Besides Madame Messiaen, other notable interpreters include John Ogdon, Paul Crossley and Robert Sherlaw Johnson.

With the works of Messiaen, the keyboard known to Bach, Mozart and Liszt appears to have exhausted its traditional role. The piano is now thumped, twanged, ceremonially demolished, and even – in John Cage's *4′ 33″* – ritually silenced. (It is difficult to applaud such an experiment without the aid of a good chronometer.) At the same time it is impossible to imagine a musical future without the keyboard, which has been to so many a solace, a sometimes infuriating challenge, an entire home orchestra and a lifetime's delight.

John Cage *(above)* sometimes requires the pianist to 'prepare' a piano in this bizarre manner. **Rick Wakeman** *(below)* records by the superimposition of several tracks

Claudio Arrau has made a brilliant record of Chopin's rarely heard variations on Mozart's *Là ci darem* from *Don Giovanni*

ALBERT AMMONS (1907–49)

American jazz pianist. He began his career playing in clubs in the Chicago area. His own band, which he formed in 1934, ran till 1938, when he moved to New York and teamed up with Pete Johnson. The last ten years of his life were marred by accident and illness. In 1941 he sliced off the top of a finger while making a sandwich, which put him out of business for a while. Later Ammons suffered increasingly from paralysis of the hands. Having overcome this handicap, he had only been playing for about a year when he was overtaken by his terminal illness. He has recorded with Count Basie, Benny Green and Woody Herman. His son Gene (Jug) was a renowned tenor saxophone player.

GEZA ANDA (1921–76)

Hungarian-born pianist. Anda studied with Dohnányi in Budapest and won the Liszt prize there. During the Second World War he escaped from Hungary and settled in Switzerland, taking Swiss citizenship in 1955. His American debut with the New York Philharmonic Orchestra took place the same year.

Anda's concert programmes contrast Romantic and modern works; it was originally for his interpretations of Brahms, Liszt and, more particularly, Bartók that he became established. Later he turned to Mozart, of which his early performances were severely criticized, not so much for a lack of technique but for a lack of understanding of the style. The pianist who could play the three formidably difficult Bartók concertos in one evening's performance seemed to have met his match in the less demanding Mozart scores. Instead of being disheartened by criticism, he applied himself assiduously (in Salzburg) to the study of Mozart, and eventually achieved a very special understanding of the music. He conducts Mozart concertos from the keyboard, an approach which has its disadvantages, for the pianist has to be on the move the whole time – but these are more than compensated for by the unity which comes from treating

the whole orchestra and keyboard as a single instrument. He can be heard directing several of Mozart's concertos with the Salzburg Mozarteum Camerata Academica on a series of albums.

MARTHA ARGERICH (1941...)

Argentinian pianist. Extraordinarily gifted as a child, Martha Argerich astonished audiences when she was only sixteen by her technical mastery of many major works, including Mozart concertos. She has an acute ear, a phenomenal memory – and an extraordinary ability to parody the styles of other pianists. However, like character actors who are able to play many parts, she seems to have had difficulty in developing a stable style of her own. In spite of the occasionally unpredictable nature of her performances, Argerich has a formidable talent, evinced by winning international prizes in the face of fierce competition. She is heard to brilliant effect in the Brahms and Liszt rhapsodies that she has recorded, or in the Prokofiev *Toccata*, Op. 11.

CLAUDIO ARRAU (1903...)

Chilean pianist. The success of Arrau's first recital at the age of five aroused such interest that he was given a grant to study in Berlin. During 1914–15 he gave recitals in Germany and Scandinavia, and made his first European tour after the First World War. He returned to South America in 1921, making his debut in the United States two years later. He enjoys all the challenges that touring brings, and believes that the continual change of environment prevents his outlook and technique from going stale. Arrau's playing is particularly noted for the clarity of inner parts; he is able to snatch motifs from the accompanying texture which throw new light on the familiar sounds of well-known classics. But when the occasion demands, as with the cadenza of the Grieg Concerto, he can be as turbulent as the most extrovert player. He has recorded extensively, making a special study of Schumann, Chopin and, particularly, Beethoven. There are various recordings of him playing the Beethoven piano concertos; his cycle of all five with the Amsterdam Concertgebouw under Bernard Haitink has been especially praised.

VLADIMIR ASHKENAZY (1937...)

Russian-born pianist. Ashkenazy was born in Gorky and, as both his parents were pianists, he received his earliest tuition at home. He went to the Central School of Music in Moscow, and later attended the Conservatoire there. He soon came into prominence winning prizes at the world's music festivals:

Daniel Barenboim is renowned for his phenomenal memory. He knows most of the standard concerto repertoire by heart

the second prize at the International Chopin competition in Warsaw when only nineteen, then first prize at the international competition in Belgium the following year, and finally the coveted Tchaikovsky Prize, of which he was a joint winner in 1962.

Ashkenazy is an ardent champion of the music of Scriabin, and frequently tries to persuade concert organizers and agents to let him include works by that composer in his programmes. Listeners for whom Scriabin is too demanding find much to admire in his performance of Rachmaninov's Third Piano Concerto, which he infuses with a tragic quality, or in his many Chopin recordings. Ashkenazy has now taken up residence in Iceland, his wife's native country.

STEFAN ASKENASE (1896...)

Polish pianist. Lwow, Askenase's birthplace, was where he received his first musical training, before moving to Vienna to study under Emil von Sauer. This was at the beginning of the First World War, and his work with Sauer was interrupted by conscription, only resuming in 1919. His debut in Vienna was in December of that year, following which he gave a recital in his native Poland before embarking on a concert tour. He then spent a few years in Cairo as a teacher at the Conservatoire, and taught in Brussels, Hamburg, Cologne and Jerusalem. During these nomadic years he found time to record extensively.

Askenase is not just a master of the piano, but of the *pianissimo*. His lyrical style is ideally suited to gentle, introspective pieces such as Chopin's *Berceuse* or the F minor Ballade, which he paints in fresh, unexpected colours. His deeply felt musical personality is thrown into sharp relief in recordings he has made of the two Chopin piano concertos, where he explores the reflective side of this flamboyant music.

WILHELM BACKHAUS (1884–1969)

German pianist. At nineteen, Backhaus played the Brahms B♭ major concerto under Hans Richter; although that performance was not recorded, Backhaus's recollections of it, his interpretation and his detailed analysis of the playing have been recalled in later performances. He toured the United States in 1912-14, and at that time was considered to be a player of the Romantic school; it could not have been foreseen that he would later be acclaimed as one of the greatest interpreters of Beethoven. He recorded the complete cycle of sonatas, and these were for a long time regarded as the definitive versions – until at the age of eighty he began to record the complete cycle once again. The second cycle was almost complete – the majestic *Hammerklavier* being the only one left to record – when he collapsed and died of a heart attack during a performance. A comparison of the two series reveals much about the development of a great pianist's intellectual approach to the music.

PAUL BADURA SKODA (1927...)

Austrian pianist. He was born in Vienna and brought up by his stepfather, in recognition of which Paul Badura added Skoda to his name. At University he studied mathematics and engineering as well as music, and by the time he was in his early twenties began to win international prizes for his playing; he toured Europe in 1952 and North America the following year.

His training in mathematics and engineering gave him some grounding into the mechanical side of pianism, and he carefully researched the sound qualities of the instruments contemporary with Mozart and later classical composers. Because the instruments of Mozart's day had thinner strings and, as a consequence, a much clearer sound, Badura-Skoda concluded that Mozart's music should be treated in a much cleaner and detached style than was usually the case. It is sometimes said that his approach to the keyboard is too modest, too reserved. But his playing too of such demanding works as the fugue from Beethoven's Opus 106 (the *Hammerklavier* sonata) is an immense *tour de force*.

DANIEL BARENBOIM (1942...)

Israeli pianist and conductor. Born in Argentina, Barenboim at first studied with his mother and father. He was later to have lessons from Edwin Fischer and study conducting with Igor Markevich. His studies were completed by a period with Nadia Boulanger. He was only seven years old when he made his first public appearance in Buenos Aires, and he appeared at Salzburg two years later. His first American performance was given with Leopold Stokowski at the Carnegie Hall in 1957. Ten years later he married the cellist Jacqueline Du Pré. He is now resident in Israel, where his family settled in 1952.

Barenboim is justly celebrated both as a conductor and as an interpreter of Beethoven, on whose music he has made some interesting comments. It is his view that an authentic Beethoven style is less a matter of imitating the sound of a Beethoven piano than of trying to re-create the kind of atmosphere that must have been there in Beethoven's own day, when the ten-

Eubie Blake *(left)* is the last surviving giant of ragtime. **Busoni** *(below)*, one of the keyboard giants of all time. By the age of fifteen he was already a veteran of the concert platform, without assistance and encouragement from any worthwhile teacher. *Right:* The beautiful **Teresa Carreño**, who, at the age of twelve, rejected the opportunity offered her of having piano lessons from Liszt. But when she was nearly forty she married Liszt's last great pupil, Eugen d'Albert

sions brought about by the startling rhythms and dissonances would have had an electric effect on his audiences.

LAZAR BERMAN (1930...)

Russian pianist. Berman's career had rather a shaky start, for although he graduated from the Moscow Conservatoire in 1953 it was not until 1970, after an Italian tour, that he made any great impression. By 1976, however, when he toured the USA for the first time, he was being received with tremendous enthusiasm. His personal choice of music leans towards to Romantic composers, especially Liszt, whose *Transcendental Studies* and *Hungarian Rhapsody No 3* he plays to great effect. Of the Russian composers, Scriabin's *Études* and the Prokofiev *Toccata* demonstrate how well he can tackle music which is both technically and intellectually demanding.

EDWARD POWER BIGGS (1906–77)

American organist. E. Power Biggs was born in Essex, England, and studied at the Royal Academy of Music in London. He was invited to play at Harvard University, where he performed all Bach's organ works in a series of ten recitals. Weekly broadcasts of organ music soon made him a familiar figure to American audiences, but he is also widely known for his editions of early organ music, as well as his efforts to promote contemporary American music for the organ. Biggs adopted American citizenship in 1938.

EUBIE BLAKE (1883...)

American jazz pianist and composer. Blake began his career playing the organ. Having had lessons from the conductor of the Baltimore Colored Symphony, Llewellyn Wilson, he won a national piano competition and became an instant bar-room celebrity. The biggest step of his career was when he teamed up with Noble Sissle to write the music for such shows as *Shuffle Along* and *Chocolate Dandies*, and soon made his name as a composer with 'I'm just wild about Harry' and 'Love will find a way', for example.

Eubie Blake faded from the musical scene for a few years, to re-emerge in 1969 and form his own record company three years later. On his ninetieth birthday he was honoured by ASCAP (The American Society of Composers, Authors and Publishers), and a few months later made the first aeroplane journey of his life. This was to be the first of many historic moments for the grand old man, others being an appearance with the Boston Pops, and the book (with tape) *Reminiscences with Sissle and Blake*. He can be heard on the albums of *Wizard of Ragtime, 86 years of Eubie Blake* and *Rags to Classics*.

ALFRED BRENDEL (1931...)

Austrian pianist. Brendel was privileged to have among his teachers such great musicians as Edwin Fischer and Paul Baumgartner. His first recital was in Graz in 1948. He toured with the Vienna Chamber Orchestra three years later, and with the Vienna Symphony Orchestra in 1954. His debut with the Vienna Philharmonic Orchestra was in 1960, and he subsequently made regular appearances with them. His interpretations of Beethoven and other classical composers were regarded as far more intelligent and exciting than any of his contemporaries' performances. If he had a fault, it was a tendency to try too hard to be 'interesting'. He revels in technical problems, and can summon up tremendous power. Apart from his Beethoven playing, Brendel's recording of the Schubert 'Wanderer' Fantasy is an outstanding performance.

DAVE BRUBECK (1920...)

American jazz pianist and composer. He learned the piano and the cello as a young boy, and started playing hillbilly jazz when he was thirteen. He studied music at the College of the Pacific, where he formed a twelve-piece band, and at Mills College, Oakland, under Darius Milhaud.

In 1949 he formed a trio and made his first recording. Then in 1951 he formed the famous quartet which (with the saxophonist Paul Desmond as an outstanding soloist) toured Europe in 1958 and 1959. They played with the New York Philharmonic Orchestra under Leonard Bernstein in his brother Howard Brubeck's *Dialogue for Jazz Combo and Orchestra*. In 1967 the group broke up, and Brubeck formed another quartet, this time with Gerry Mulligan (sax), Jack Six (bass) and Alan Dawson (drums). By the time Mulligan left in 1972, Brubeck's own sons were ready to step into the quartet's shoes, and with Darius, Danny and Chris he recorded *Two Generations of Brubeck*.

Brubeck's music and playing is quite individual; to the classical jibe that all jazz was in 4/4 time he responded with the renowned *Time Out* album, with pieces in all kinds of complex rhythms. 'Blue Rondo a la Turk', perhaps the most outstanding, is very reminiscent of Bartók's music. Brubeck's improvisatory style is best heard in 'Over the Rainbow'. He has also written some extended works, which include an oratorio, *The Light in the Wilderness*.

FERRUCCIO BUSONI (1866–1924)

Italian pianist and composer. He was first taught by his parents, who were both musical; although he attended the Vienna Conservatoire, he later claimed that he had learnt nothing there. For a while he studied at Leipzig, and later was professor of piano in Helsinki (where he came into contact with Sibelius and Järnefelt). He toured the United States in 1891 and taught in Boston for a time before settling in Berlin, playing and teaching.

His playing was in the grand Lisztian tradition, but without any sentimentality. Chopin, Liszt and Bach (many of whose organ works he transcribed) were treated alike: 'Bach', he said, 'is the foundation of piano playing. Liszt is the summit.'

He made few recordings: the evidence is that he hated making gramophone records, and that the results do not indicate what his true style was like. The restriction on playing time prevented Busoni from building up to his full capabilities, apart from the fact that in the early days of recordings, every note played remained for posterity – always an unnerving consideration.

Busoni composed a considerable amount of music; among his pieces are a formidable piano concerto, three operas and an incomplete fourth (Dr Faustus), which is regarded as his greatest work. Two years before his death he complained, 'I have devoted myself too much to Bach, Mozart and Liszt. I wish now that I could emancipate myself from them.'

C

TERESA CARRENO (1853–1917)

Venezuelan pianist. Talented, beautiful and tempestuous, Teresa Carreño was long regarded as the Queen of the piano. As a talented girl of nine she was heard by Gottschalk, who proclaimed her a genius. The following year she played before President Lincoln – and complained about the piano. At thirteen she made a deep impression on both Rossini and Liszt, one wanted to teach her singing, the other the piano. She did neither, but had occasional lessons from both Adelina Patti and Anton Rubinstein whenever her busy concert tours allowed her. She often sang, taking the parts of the Queen in *Les Huguenots* and Zerlina in *Don Giovanni*, and even conducted on occasions.

Her violent personality, especially the turbulent relationship she had with her third husband, the equally volatile Eugen D'Albert, was notorious. However, her time with D'Albert certainly made her a better artist to judge from contemporary accounts. Her final marriage, to the brother of her second husband, while causing something of a scandal, turned out to be her happiest.

Carreño tackled and mastered the 'big' concertos: Liszt, Rubinstein and Tchaikovsky. She was one of the first pianists to play the Grieg Concerto (though the composer did not take kindly to her embellishments) and gave the première of her pupil MacDowell's D minor concerto.

ROBERT CASADESUS (1899–1972)

French pianist and composer. Casadesus' musical family included his uncles François (a conductor and composer), Henri (a violinist) and an Aunt Rose, who was a pianist. He studied at the Paris Conservatoire, winning prizes in 1913, 1919 and 1921.

Alfred Cortot loved the music of Wagner. It is said that he could play the scores of all the operas from memory

He began touring the following year, making a name first for interpretations that were lyrical, charming and modest. At the outbreak of the Second World War he went to the United States, where he also lectured. Among his many compositions are symphonies and concertos, including one for two pianos, which received its first performance in Warsaw in 1934 and which he played with his wife Gaby and the New York Philharmonic Orchestra in 1940.

His later playing moved away from the earlier lyricism into a much more powerful, almost aggressive style – it was criticized accordingly. The pendulum having swung to the other side, he returned to a balance of refined judgement; his recordings of Mozart and Ravel are beautifully poised and lyrical.

VAN CLIBURN (1934…)

American pianist. Born in Shreveport, Louisiana, Van Cliburn was the first American to win the coveted Tchaikovsky Prize. His early tuition was given almost exclusively by his mother, who had been a pupil of Arthur Friedheim (himself a pupil of Liszt), and he later attended the Juilliard School of Music.

His first performance of the Tchaikovsky B♭ minor concerto, which he played with the Houston Symphony Orchestra, was given when he was only twelve years old. He played it again with the New York Philharmonic for his debut there in 1954. In spite of this most impressive beginning, he remained in comparative obscurity. It was not until 1957, when he had returned to Texas to look after his ailing mother, that his teacher persuaded him to enter the Moscow competition. His success there, which included being kissed by Khrushchev, made him an internationally known figure overnight. But it was his playing of significantly difficult solo works which brought him to the attention of the judges. His success in the Tchaikovsky and Rachmaninov concertos had the unfortunate effect of almost confining him to these works for the remainder of his concert career.

ALFRED CORTOT (1877–1962)

French pianist and conductor. Born in Switzerland of French parents, Cortot studied at the Paris Conservatoire with Dièmer. He became active in a wide field of musical enterprises; having been an assistant conductor at Bayreuth, he was filled with the enthusiasm to conduct Wagner in Paris, and also to fill a void by founding a choral society, La Société de Festival Lyrique, and the École Normale de Musique. He was responsible for the first performances in Paris of such works as *Götterdämmerung*, *Parsifal*, Brahms' *German Requiem* and Beethoven's *Mass in D*. He was also interested in the mechanical reproduction of music on the pianola, and when Martenot invented his electronic *Ondes*, wrote the preface to a manual for it. As a writer, he produced the *Rational Principles of Pianoforte Technique*, and analysed difficult passages to find the best ways of overcoming technical problems in *Daily Keyboard Gymnastics*. With all this activity, it is a wonder that he had any time to practise. It has to be admitted that there were wrong notes and slips of memory, but so great was the esteem in which Cortot was held, that one accepted these flaws as irritations, like scratches on a record.

In spite of his having been created a Commandeur de la Légion d'honneur there was some feeling running against him after the Second World War, connected with his having accepted the post of the Paris Radio Orchestra conductorship. He gave a final tour in 1952 and retired to Lausanne in Switzerland. Several of the many recordings Cortot made, of solo and chamber music, have been reissued to the delight of collectors.

CLIFFORD CURZON (1907…)

English pianist. Born in London, Curzon studied at the Royal Academy of Music, where he also taught for a while from 1926. Among his teachers were Tobias Matthay, Artur Schnabel and Wanda Landowska. He made regular appearances at the famous promenade concerts; in fact his debut at them was in the Queen's Hall (now demolished), where he played in Bach's Triple Concerto at the age of sixteen. His first tour abroad was as accompanist to the viola player Lionel Tertis in a pilot scheme organized by the British Council, and he later went to Paris with the BBC orchestra to play the solo part in Constant Lambert's *Rio Grande*. His American debut was in New York in 1939, where he would have settled but for the war. He remained in England for the duration, then returned to the United States in 1947.

Sir Clifford Curzon's training as an ensemble player and as an accompanist has made his performances in chamber music exceptionally sensitive. Though a virtuoso, he avoids display for its own sake, as his recording of the Brahms Piano Quintet with the Budapest String Quartet reveals.

In 1933 he married Lucille Wallace, the American harpsichordist, with whom he has given frequent recitals.

CARL CZERNY (1791–1857)

Viennese pianist, teacher and composer. He was a pupil of Beethoven and the teacher of Liszt and Leschetizky as well as other important pianists. His first lessons were from his father, a Bohemian music teacher who had settled in Vienna. When Carl was nine he was introduced to Beethoven by a friend of the composer. Hearing the boy play the *Pathétique* Sonata, Beethoven decided to accept him as a pupil. Later, Beethoven wrote a testimonial for him which spoke in glowing terms of the boy's capabilities and progress, and referred to his phenomenal memory.

It is as a teacher that Czerny is best known, and also for his books of exercises which have been the foundation of many a pianist's technique. These run to many volumes, but are somewhat dry and colourless – and were even regarded as such in his day. Chopin, who visited him in Vienna, wrote afterwards that Czerny was a good deal warmer than his music.

Among Czerny's innumerable compositions and arrangements are versions of the orchestral overtures to Rossini's *Semiramide* and *William Tell* for sixteen pianists at eight pianos.

GYÖRGY CZIFFRA (1921...)

Hungarian pianist. Cziffra's early career was as a cabaret and cafe pianist. Later, when he became a recital pianist, he specialized in Romantic works, especially those of Liszt. His musical education was interrupted by the war; he later escaped from Hungary during the 1956 uprising. His playing is personal in that he sometimes lets his personality override many traditionally accepted methods of interpretation. He can be heard at his best in Liszt's *Totentanz*, which he plays with tremendous zest, and the *Hungarian Fantasia*, where he is more pensive. Highly recommended is his performance in the César Franck *Symphonic Variations*. Cziffra is in addition a highly persuasive exponent of the unfashionable practice of playing early music on the piano. He has recorded sparkling versions of Couperin, Rameau, Lully, and in particular of that most pianistic of all the harpsichord composers, Domenico Scarlatti.

Czerny was one of music's most prolific composers. His list of opus numbers reaches almost to 1000

The playing of **Clifford Curzon** is much revered for its exquisite shading in the pianissimo register. An outstanding example of this musical sensibility is his performance of Schumann's *Scenes from Childhood* (*Kinderscenen*, op. 15)

Eugen d'Albert wrote twenty operas, in addition to his busy life as a travelling virtuoso and teacher of renown

EUGEN D'ALBERT (1864–1932)

Pianist and composer. Although d'Albert was brought up in Britain and studied at what is now the Royal College of Music in London, he went to Vienna to continue his studies and then progressed to Weimar. He considered Germany rather than England to be his home; at the age of twenty he wrote that he had learnt nothing in 'that land of fogs'. His temperament was volatile and testy, reflected in his private life – he was married seven times, once to the pianist Teresa Carreño (who was herself three times a bride). In his prime he was a brilliant pianist. Liszt paid him the highest compliment he could think of, which was 'a second Tausig'. Bruno Walter referred to his playing as 'titanic'. The epithet was apt; his career as a pianist was short, and he turned to composing music which is now seldom revived. Occasional recordings of his playing are discovered, but they were obviously made at a time when his technique had sunk without trace. The composer-pianist Dohnányi studied with him for a while.

JEANNE DEMESSIEUX (1921–68)

French organist and composer. At the age of twelve, Jeanne Demessieux was already playing at the church of Saint-Esprit, Paris. Later she went to the Paris Conservatoire, where she studied with Marcel Dupré. In 1952 she became professor of organ at the conservatoire in Liège, and toured the United States the following year.

She was particularly renowned for the excellence of her improvisation, as well as for her ability as a composer. Her performances of her own compositions *Prelude and Fugue in C* for organ and *Poème* for organ and orchestra have been recorded.

JÖRG DEMUS (1928…)

Austrian pianist. Demus studied at the Vienna Staatsakademie from 1940 to 1945. Among his teachers were the renowned Walter Gieseking and Edwin Fischer; he also studied conducting under Josef Krips. His debut was in 1943 with the Gesellschaft der Musikfreunde, Vienna. Once the dust of the war had settled, he took the opportunity to travel, and from 1948 toured Europe widely. His American debut was in 1955, and the following year he succeeded in winning the international Busoni Prize in Bolzano, Italy. He is regarded as one of the finest of the school of Viennese pianists, who had to study under the most difficult conditions. He specializes in the works of Beethoven, which he sometimes plays on the fortepiano.

MARCEL DUPRÉ (1886–1971)

French organist. Born in Rouen, Dupré was a prodigiously gifted child. At the age of ten he could play Bach's Preludes and Fugues from memory; by the time he was twelve he had already written an oratorio, *Le Songe de Jacob* (*Jacob's Dream*). At the Paris Conservatoire he proved to be one of the most brilliant students. He won prizes in piano playing in 1905, and the following year Widor invited him to be his assistant at Saint-Sulpice. He took more prizes: for organ playing in 1907, for fugue (in Widor's class) in 1909 and finally the Grand Prix de Rome in 1914. In 1916 he became organist at Notre Dame in Paris, owing to the ill-health of the previous organist, Louis Vierne.

He astonished listeners both by his amazing improvisations and his phenomenal memory; he could play the whole of Bach's organ music from memory. In 1920 he visited London for the first time in his recital career and appeared at the Royal Albert Hall. After that, the war years excluded, he visited England almost every year to perform. A close friend of Sir Henry Wood, he made frequent appearances at the Handel Festivals held in the 1930s, playing Wood's arrangements of the Handel organ concertos (most of which are written for organ without pedals, but with string orchestra accompaniment) for pedal organ.

Dupré's own compositions are extremely complex, both to hear and to play. The exceptions are the teaching pieces *Le Tombeau de Titelouze*, a series of seventy-nine chorales. He has also written a quantity of choral music, notably a magnificent *De Profundis* for solo voices with chorus, orchestra and, of course, organ.

DUKE ELLINGTON (1899–1974)

Jazz composer, pianist and arranger. During the 1920s, jazz took a direction that was virtually a contradiction of its own definition: the formation of big bands with sections rather than individual instruments. Written-down arrangements tore apart the concept that jazz was an improvised, spontaneous sound. With Duke Ellington there came another break with tradition. He can be regarded as the first (and greatest) jazz composer.

He formed a band in his mid-twenties and wrote with the players in mind, so preserving the distinctive tone-colours of the musicians he had assembled. The Ellington sound remained distinctive because of the loyalty and respect that everyone felt for him: one of his players, Harry Carney, who joined him at the outset, stayed with him for the rest of his life – a forty-seven-year partnership.

Ellington separated jazz music from its cat-house origins and attained standards that were admired by the greatest artists of his day, among them Leopold Stokowski, Igor Stravinsky and Percy Grainger.

CHRISTOPH ESCHENBACH (1940...)

German pianist. Born in Breslau, Eschenbach's studies took him to Aachen, Cologne, and eventually to Hamburg, where he studied with Hans Schmidt-Neuhaus and Eliza Hauser. His prizes included the Munich International Competition in 1962, and the Clara Haskil Prize in Cologne, 1965. The following year he was signed up by Deutsche Grammophon, for whom he has made over fifty recordings. The same year he made his debut in London, first appearing as a soloist at the Festival Hall, then with the London Symphony Orchestra, playing the concerto which Hans Werne Henze wrote for him.

He is best known for his interpretations of the Romantics, from Beethoven to Brahms. Since 1978 he has been making appearances as a conductor.

Christoph Eschenbach *(left)* has a clarity in his playing that is ideally suited to chamber music and the neglected medium of piano duet. **Duke Ellington** *(above)* was considered by no less a musician than Percy Grainger to have been one of the three greatest composers, along with J. S. Bach and Frederick Delius

RUDOLF FIRKUŠNY (1912...)

Czech-born pianist, now resident in America. Firkušny studied at the Brno Conservatoire, where, in addition to his piano studies, he was taught theory by Janáček. While at Brno he appeared, at the age of sixteen, as a soloist in his own piano concerto. In 1928 he moved to Prague and graduated the following year. He toured Europe, but did not visit the USA until several years later. When he did, he took the opportunity to study for a while with Artur Schnabel. Although he eventually settled in the USA in 1940, he returned to Czechoslovakia after the war to give concerts in Prague and Brno.

Among his recordings are the complete works of Janáček, on whose music he is an authority. Reference has already been made to Firkušny's ability as a composer, and since his early concerto he has written a number of piano pieces of considerable difficulty.

ANNIE FISCHER (1914...)

Hungarian pianist. Annie Fischer amazed the musical public of Budapest with her performance of the Beethoven C major concerto when she was only eight years old. By the time she was twelve she had made appearances outside her own country, impressing all who heard her by her mastery of the instrument and her interpretation of the music. She studied at the Liszt Academy in Budapest, one of her teachers being Erno Dohnányi, and became the best pupil of the Academy. In 1933, the youngest of a hundred contestants, she won the Liszt International Piano Competition. During the war she remained in Sweden, returning afterwards to Budapest.

She has played under many famous conductors; her first appearance in the USA was with George Szell, playing Mozart's Concerto K.482; it was well received, although critics commented that her performance showed a lack of eighteenth-century scholarship. In spite of that initial reservation, she has now acquired a formidable reputation and has appeared at the world's leading music festivals. She has been awarded Hungary's highest accolade, the Kossuth Prize, three times.

EDWIN FISCHER (1886–1960)

Swiss pianist and conductor. Fischer's early studies were in his native city of Basle. He taught at the Stern Conservatoire in Berlin for a while, then began a period of concert work. His playing was renowned not only for its technique but for the intelligence of his approach to the music.

Between the wars he was regarded as a distinguished interpreter of Beethoven, but this was followed by his acquiring a reputation for the music of Bach. It was to be expected that he should turn to conducting. His performances may seem unscholarly by present-day criteria, but at the time were authoritative. For example, his recording of Bach's Second Brandenburg Concerto uses a harpsichord continuo, authentically enough, but in his version of the Fifth Concerto he conducts (and plays the solo part) from the piano. Authentic or not, his recording of the Bach F minor keyboard concerto must be one of the most convincing Bach performances of the century.

VIRGIL FOX (1912...)

American organist. He was head of the organ department of Peabody Conservatory in Baltimore from 1938 to 1942, and organist at the Riverside Church, New York, from 1946 to 1964. Fox took a Romantic approach to Baroque music and usually played at a fast (sometimes very fast) tempo, which was always sparklingly clear, but not always in the spirit of the work.

ERROLL GARNER (1921–74)

American jazz pianist and composer. The composer of the jazz-classic 'Misty' was born in Pittsburgh, Pennsylvania. Until 1944 he spent his time developing his piano talent locally, but in his mid-twenties went to seek his fortune in New York. His easy style, reminiscent of Fats Waller, attracted audiences who were not converted jazz fans. Garner played with small groups which could provide a background to highlight his particular brand of playing, in which left-hand spread chords provide a guitar-like accompaniment to rapid figurations in the right.

He never bothered to learn to read music, his compositions being taken down by dictation.

FERNANDO GERMANI (1906...)

Italian organist. The respected teacher, Germani, is also highly regarded as a concert virtuoso. His studies in Rome were followed by a period at the Pontifical Institute of Sacred Music. His teaching appointments have taken him from Rome and Siena to the Curtis Institute in Philadelphia. He was four years old when he gave his first public recital, and at the age of fifteen was appointed assistant organist of the Augusto Symphony Orchestra. He made his debut at London's Royal Albert Hall in 1936, playing a programme that covered a wide range of music. His own preferences include very early organ music – particularly Frescobaldi – but he has also done a great deal to introduce Italian audiences to the music of Reger.

WALTER GIESEKING (1895–1956)

Franco-German pianist. Born in France to German parents, Gieseking

Godowsky *(left)* wrote piano transcriptions of unparalleled complexity. **Gottschalk** *(below)* left a garrulous volume of memoirs, *Notes of a Pianist*, containing much sharp observation and a keen sense of humour

was one product of the German school who specialized in the French Impressionists. Certainly his reputation grew out of his extraordinary ability to play gradations of sound from *pp* to *ppp*. Ravel and Debussy 'spoke through his fingers', it has been said.

He saw no necessity to go to school; he could play the piano at four, and at five he could read and write. At eleven he entered the Hanover Conservatoire, and at fifteen played all Beethoven's sonatas in a series of six recitals – between four and six sonatas at each concert! He had an amazing memory and coupled this with excellent sight-reading (it is often said that the two are mutually exclusive) – and having mastered a composition, needed to do little practice. 'Only dirty people need to wash,' was his caustic comment.

EMIL GILELS (1916...)

Russian pianist. Gilels was born in Odessa, and gave his first recital there at the age of thirteen. Less than four years later he took first prize in an All-Union music competition, and went on to take the first prizes in international competitions in Vienna and Brussels. His European concert debut was in 1954 in Paris, and he later appeared with the Philadelphia Orchestra under Eugene Ormandy.

He is now regarded as one of the world's leading pianists in the Russian Romantic tradition, displaying all the sparkling virtuosity of the Lisztian school. He has recorded a vast repertoire and can be heard to brilliant effect in music which ranges from Scarlatti sonatas to Saint-Saëns' second piano concerto.

He has twice received the Order of Lenin, as well as honours from other countries for his outstanding contributions to music, particularly with his record as the first pianist from behind the Iron Curtain to play in the USA.

LEOPOLD GODOWSKY (1870–1938)

American pianist. Godowsky was originally Lithuanian and, apart from some instruction from local teachers, was virtually self-taught. He had an extraordinary ear and memory; having heard a brass band play a piece when he was three, he played it on the piano a year later without ever having heard the music since, nor having had piano lessons. He was eventually sent to Berlin to study, and later went on tour with a violinist as an accompanist. He met Saint-Saëns shortly afterwards, and though they became friends, Godowsky discounted any idea that Saint-Saëns might have given him lessons in piano playing.

It is remarkable, then, that Godowsky should have developed a technique that was envied by all who heard him. His Berlin debut was in 1900; the hall was packed, and Godowsky astonished himself as much as anyone by playing brilliantly – the audience went wild.

He was a shy, retiring man, and disliked giving concerts. Perhaps because he lacked flamboyancy and magnetism, he was less successful with the general public than with his fellow musicians. It was well known that Godowsky played at his most brilliant when in less formal surroundings than the concert hall.

He believed in no particular method; in fact the title of a paper he wrote was 'The best method is eclectic'. A rare recording, made in 1928, of the Grieg *Ballade*, shows his playing to outstanding effect.

LOUIS MOREAU GOTTSCHALK (1829–69)

American pianist and composer. Born in New Orleans of a French mother and English father, he had outstripped local teachers by the time he was twelve, and was sent to Paris to study. Three years later the young Gottschalk, wealthy, handsome and with impeccable manners, made his debut at the Salon Pleyel. Chopin and Kalkbrenner, both present, were impressed by the young musician. Probably Gottschalk could have gone on to be one of the greatest pianists of his age; but the novelty of his nationality, coupled with the exotic sounds of his new compositions, assured him of a fashionable audience and comfortable living.

His New York debut was in 1853. After making an initial hit, the young lion fell foul of the critic John Sullivan Dwight, who quite rightly criticized his performances for their lack of substance, his programmes consisting, as they did, exclusively of his own compositions. Furious, at a later concert Gottschalk substituted one of Beethoven's Bagatelles for the advertised piece on the programme – and told no one. Not even Dwight noticed the substitution, which did little to endear them to each other.

In adopting jazz rhythms and the sounds of banjo strumming in his

music, Gottschalk virtually founded an American school and forged a bridge, as it were, between the salon music of Chopin and the gritty cat-house rags of Scott Joplin. Unfortunately his salon pieces such as 'The Dying Poet' and 'The Last Hope' display not so much naïveté as shallowness. By all accounts his playing was delicate, often likened to shimmering silver, but he frequently resorted to simplifying passages he was unable to execute. His nail-biting was such that blood-spattered keys were often gruesome witnesses to this pianistically inexpedient habit. He died, after a short but eventful life, during an extended tour of South America, in the most unsavoury circumstances.

In performance **Glenn Gould** sits low on the piano stool, an approach which requires an exceptionally strong finger technique

GLENN GOULD (1932…)

Canadian pianist. Gould attended the conservatory in Toronto, and was one of the youngest students to graduate – being only twelve years old at the time. He made his debut two years later with the Toronto Symphony Orchestra. Gould's playing is highly personal, almost as if he refuses to be intimidated by scholars and pedants. Undaunted by comments from purists, he has made a point of playing Bach on the piano, often using tempi which defy accepted practice.

His playing goes from one extreme to the other – from a demonic *bravura* to the most tortine of *adagios* – but the impression is always one of justification. His recordings include all Mozart's piano sonatas, and a number of twentieth-century standard works, such as Alban Berg's Piano Sonata and a number of pieces by Schoenberg. Also recommended for the listener who appreciates something out of the usual is his performance of Richard Strauss's *Enoch Arden* with narration by the actor Claude Rains. His public performances are rare, his temperament not being at one with the concert platform. Gould prefers the ambience of the recording studio; his intelligent, if mannered, recordings of Bach's keyboard music more than bear out this eccentric preference.

PERCY GRAINGER (1882–1961)

Australian composer and pianist. Grainger the composer of light salon pieces has eclipsed Grainger the pianist. Ironically, it was money earned from recital work in Australia that enabled him to study in Germany, where he was a pupil of Busoni. Another influence in his life was to be Edvard Grieg, whose Piano Concerto became a standard part of Grainger's repertoire.

His interest in modernism led him to be a foremost exponent of new music, including Debussy, Albéniz and Delius. His playing had an easy freedom which brought sweetness and clarity, even to heavy transcriptions.

He was regarded as a mild eccentric of the vegetarian wholefood variety. These oddities spilled into his own compositions, with some remarkable instructions to the pianist (in the vernacular). These compositions (such as 'Country Gardens') had a certain vogue but were really in the same class as the mid-nineteenth-century transcriptions of popular airs. Sadly, these have become the legacy for which he is best known, and have eclipsed his finer miniatures. Grainger's proficiency as a pianist can be judged in re-issues of his playing Liszt, Schumann and his own works.

Percy Grainger loved the English countryside, a feeling that is apparent in his numerous transcriptions of folk dances. He was known to have gone on tour there on foot, walking from one concert to another with a knapsack on his back. His eccentric ways must have made his manager extremely nervous

INGRID HAEBLER (1929...)

Austrian pianist. This brilliant exponent of the Viennese school has a formidable list of achievements. After her early training at the Salzburg Mozarteum and periods of study at the conservatoires of Vienna, Geneva and Paris, Ingrid Haebler went on to win first prizes at international piano competitions in Munich and Geneva. She was very much in demand as a recording artist, and took the Grand Prix du Disque in 1958. Her early career tended to centre round the Romantics – Schubert, Chopin and Schumann – but it was for her interpretations of Mozart that she became internationally renowned. The seal of authority was conferred on her when she was awarded the Festival Prize at Salzburg in 1964; five years later she was the recipient of the Mozart Medal in Vienna.

Apart from her Romantic recordings, including all Chopin's Nocturnes, she has recorded the complete Mozart piano sonatas and concertos. Recently she has turned her attentions to lesser-known music, such as the works of Johann Christian Bach, played on the fortepiano with crystalline clarity.

CLARA HASKIL (1895...)

Rumanian pianist. With Rudolf Firkušny, Haskil is one of the few representatives of what might be a Central European School. Like Firkušny, her studies and influences were at the Paris Conservatoire, where she won a first prize when only fourteen. She soon established herself as a pianist, not only of quality but of distinctive temperament and approach. Her sensitivity to the music, and to other players, brought her into demand as a duo artiste, and she appeared with Ysaÿe, Enesco, Casals and Geza Anda. Her clear and expressive qualities are exemplified in her interpretations of Mozart, while her Schumann playing is highly praised for its sensibility.

ADOLF VON HENSELT (1814–89)

German pianist. Though he rarely played in public (and was an appalling teacher), Henselt must be included for the phenomenal esteem in which he was held during his lifetime, being regarded as the equal of Liszt. At his debut he suffered a lapse of memory, left the stage and could not pluck up the courage to return for a long time thereafter. When he eventually did play in public it was in a state of terror; he would hide during long orchestral *tutti* sections, then rush to the piano for his cue. Once, playing before the Tsar, he forgot to put out a cigar, and nervously puffed on it throughout the rest of his performance. Critics raved over Henselt's playing: his fingers could produce as much tone as Liszt's arms, and he had managed to increase the stretch of his palm and fingers (even though he only had small hands) so that he could play every one of the ten notes of the chord of C major over a span of three octaves. The independence of his fingers meant that he could play the music of Bach with harpsichord-like clarity. Stuffing the piano with feathers, so as not to be heard, he would play through the 48 Preludes and Fugues late into the night (at the same time reading the Bible). He terrified, rather than taught, pupils. Dressed in a white suit and red fez, he carried a fly swatter which descended with a cry of 'Wrong!' every time a mistake was made.

MYRA HESS (1890–1965)

English pianist. One of the best-loved of English musicians, Dame Myra was revered and respected for her efforts in establishing a series of midday concerts during the war for Londoners who were unable to return to the city in the evening. She began her musical studies at the Guildhall School of Music, then won a scholarship to the Royal Academy when she was seven. After five years' work with Tobias Matthay she played Beethoven's G major concerto at the Queen's Hall under Sir Thomas Beecham. Her success as a concert artist was assured, and having been acclaimed in Europe, she made her debut in the USA in 1922.

She had a wide repertoire, but was known primarily for her playing of Bach, and more particularly for her own arrangements of arias and chorales such as 'Jesu, Joy of Man's Desiring' and 'Sheep May Safely Graze'. Her playing of Mozart and Schumann was also highly admired.

EARL HINES (1905...)

American jazz pianist and composer. Both Hines's parents were musicians: his father was a trumpeter and his mother an organist. While at high school in Pittsburgh he played in a trio in clubs, and when the lack of finance meant that he had to give up his aspirations to be a concert pianist, he became accompanist to a jazz singer. He gradually moved into prominence and for a short while, in 1927, played with Louis Armstrong. This spurred him into starting his own Chicago-based band, which ran for nearly twenty years, during which time he acquired the sobriquet 'Fatha'. He teamed up with Louis Armstrong again in 1948, but after three years went back to playing with small groups.

It is remarkable that Hines's style altered very little between his earliest days (as he can be heard in Volume 3 of *The Louis Armstrong Story*) and the 1960s. His own favourite recordings are his *Second Balcony Jump*, *I Got It Bad*, and *The Earl*, all masterpieces in their particular medium.

JOSEF HOFMANN (1876–1957)

Polish pianist. One of the first pianists to insist on the sanctity of the written note, Hofmann was considered by many to be the most technically flawless player of the century. He studied at first with his father, later with Moszkowski and Anton Rubinstein.

His first concert appearance was given when he was six, and he made his debut in the United States at the age of eleven. The sensation, and successes, of his playing turned sour when the Society for the Prevention of Cruelty to Children began to investigate the enormous amount of time that the boy was spending in giving concerts and travelling America. His father suddenly cancelled all his son's concert engagements, ostensibly because of ill-health, but it soon became known that a very wealthy businessman had offered Josef's father $50,000 on condition that the boy did not give any more concerts until he was eighteen. The concert agent then initiated a summons against the father for breach of contract, but had to withdraw it when medical examination showed the young Josef to be on the verge of mental collapse.

After his studies with Rubinstein, Hofmann gave his second 'debut' in Hamburg, with Rubinstein conducting his Concerto in D minor. He renewed his concert career, settled in the United States, and in 1937 gave his most successful concert – the fiftieth anniversary of his American debut – at the Metropolitan Opera. Hofmann composed occasionally under the name of Michael Dvorsky.

VLADIMIR HOROWITZ (1904...)

Russian-born pianist. The tremendous following enjoyed by Horowitz is due to his having one of the most flawless techniques of any pianist. He was born in Kiev, and became a pupil of Felix Blumenthal, who had himself studied under Anton Rubinstein. He soon became established as a pianist, though he had originally hoped to be a composer. During 1924 he gave twenty recitals in Leningrad; in 1925 he was astounding Berlin; and in 1928 he made his American debut in the Tchaikovsky B♭ minor concerto (with Sir Thomas Beecham also making his debut there).

He was soon accepted as one of the most astonishing pianists of all. His audiences were perhaps disappointed that he made everything sound so easy, but he usually reserved some fireworks for the end of his programmes. A great favourite was his transcription of Sousa's *Stars and Stripes Forever*, which he played, in the words of one critic, 'with all three hands'.

The music came from his fingers not his wrists, arms or body. Crispness and evenness (though not necessarily depth) were the hallmarks of his Clementi or Scarlatti. He was not above adding to the printed note, *vide* his 'translation' of Mussorgsky's *Pictures at an Exhibition*. When fire and brimstone were required, it was there in his Tchaikovsky and Rachmaninov concertos. The technical and intellectual difficulties of Scriabin were mastered effortlessly. He withdrew from concert life on two occasions, once for a couple of years because of illness, and then when he officially retired in 1953. But in 1965 he emerged from retirement temporarily, to the kind of accolade usually reserved for rock stars.

Horowitz is among the most eclectic of all pianists, with a repertoire that extends from Scarlatti to Scriabin. No other performer (with the possible exception of Landowska) has played Scarlatti with such headlong accuracy. Yet the music is never scrambled, always retaining its poise

JOSÉ ITURBI (1895...)

Spanish pianist. Iturbi is the Spanish pianist who stands mid-way (in time) between Enrique Granados and Alicia de Larrocha, but musically he is much more cosmopolitan than his great compatriots. He studied in Valencia (where he was born), in Barcelona and at the Paris Conservatoire, where he gained a first prize. He taught, as head of the piano school, at the Geneva Conservatoire for a few years, but embarked on a concert career in 1923, in which year he also first appeared in England. Five years later he made his American debut as soloist with the Philadelphia Orchestra.

Once he had gained an established place as one of the world's finest pianists, he embarked on a career as a conductor. In this respect he is better known in the Americas than in Europe, where he is still primarily regarded as an outstanding pianist. Numerous film appearances tended to detract from the serious level of Iturbi's musicianship.

JAMES P. JOHNSON (1891–1955)

American jazz pianist and composer. The composer of the jazz classic 'Charleston' had his earliest lessons from his mother and local teachers. When the family moved to New York, Johnson got a job playing in clubs during his school holidays (he was just thirteen at the time). He acquired a following and, by the time the First World War broke out, had a small band going. He eventually went on the road with a couple of shows: *Dudley's Smart Set* and *Plantation Days*, which toured England and Europe. His style was essentially ragtime with a heavy and rhythmic 'stride' left hand; 'It's Love that cures the Heart's Disease' is an especially fine example of the romantic Johnson at his best. Some of his earliest playing was recorded on Aeolian piano rolls, which have now been released on disc. The ebullient 'Carolina Shout' is an early Johnson masterpiece from that time. Less known are his incursions into serious music; he has written a few symphonic jazz compositions.

EILEEN JOYCE (*c* 1912...)

Australian pianist. Because of her somewhat theatrical habit of changing her dresses between items on the programme, Eileen Joyce won large (if not discriminate) audiences, but at the same time lost the attention of serious critics. She had, nevertheless, an assured technique and a musical sensitivity which has perhaps been overlooked by some critics.

Born in Tasmania, she completed her studies at the Leipzig Conservatoire, settled in London, and by dint of hard work and craftsmanship soon made a name for herself. Her repertoire consists mainly of popular concertos, although she is adept at giving an exemplary performance of more sophisticated pieces.

FRIEDRICH KALKBRENNER (1785–1849)

German pianist. Kalkbrenner was born in a coach travelling to Berlin. His early musical training was in the hands of his father (the minor, but in his day celebrated, composer Christian Kalkbrenner). He entered the Paris Conservatoire when he was twelve, and from 1813 began to appear in public. He settled in London for nine years and became a fashionable teacher and performer.

His teaching precepts were rule-of-thumb generalizations of the kind which were in vogue at the time: varied repeats, ascending passages played *crescendo* (and *vice versa*), *rallentandi* at the end of the phrases, and so on. His own playing must have had considerable elegance and polish, for he was highly praised by eminent musicians of his day, including Hallé, who had not yet heard Chopin play, and Chopin, whom Kalkbrenner promptly offered to teach.

Nearly every report of Kalkbrenner's playing is tinged with some remark at Kalkbrenner's expense. He appears to have been an insufferable snob, claiming that he had been offered a peerage and was on the best of terms with most of the ruling families of Europe. The German poet Heine said that though Kalkbrenner affected the mannerisms of someone turned out by a confectioner, he could not disguise his backstreet origins. Chopin, Mendelssohn and Liszt (it is said) once conspired to play an elaborate trick on him. Disguising themselves as tramps, they accosted him in a fashionable cafe, where he was entertaining some society acquaintances. To his utter embarrassment they greeted him like an old friend, calling him by his first name and putting him to every conceivable kind of humiliation. Such tales, though often apocryphal, are no less of a clue to their subject's character.

JULIUS KATCHEN (1926–69)

American Pianist. A prodigious child, Katchen appeared with the Philadelphia Orchestra in New York when he was only eleven years old. He studied philosophy at Haverford College, and later confessed his gratitude to the composer Roger Sessions for having dissuaded him from studying music at university. From 1948 he toured, finding even more acclaim abroad.

He had a remarkable memory, and his repertoire included more than thirty concertos. Friends speak of his tremendous vitality and joy of living; he would practise for twelve hours, go out on the town, then be up next day at six o'clock to start all over again. He was devoted to the works of Brahms, and felt more drawn to him than any other composer. The first violin concerto he heard was by Brahms, the first time he saw Bruno Walter conduct, it was a Brahms symphony, and Katchen himself recorded all Brahms's piano music, as well as the piano trios and the accompanied cello sonatas.

WILHELM KEMPFF (1895...)

German pianist. Kempff was taught the piano by his father, and by the time he was twenty was gaining a reputation as a pianist and composer. His earlier recitals included improvisations, a feature which is nowadays almost exclusively associated either with organ performances or works of the avant-garde school.

He is now generally renowned as a great interpreter of Beethoven and Schumann; his recorded performances evince maturity rather than showmanship, and in his seemingly casual approach he interprets 'from the heart', it has been said. Critics have noticed that he sometimes separates the hands to achieve expressiveness. His duo performances with the violin-

Wilhelm Kempff is leading interpreter of the great school of German pianism

ist Yehudi Menuhin have been rightly acclaimed for the musical balance between the instruments.

WALTER KLIEN (1928...)

Austrian pianist. Born in Graz, Klien studied at the Vienna Musikakademie, and soon made his mark as a pianist of considerable prowess. He was the first pianist to record the complete solo works of Brahms, and followed this by recording the complete solo works of Mozart and all the Schubert sonatas. Above all he is a Mozart specialist, and among several international awards is the Best Mozart Record of 1970.

In 1963 he founded a duo with the violinist Wolfgang Schneiderhan.

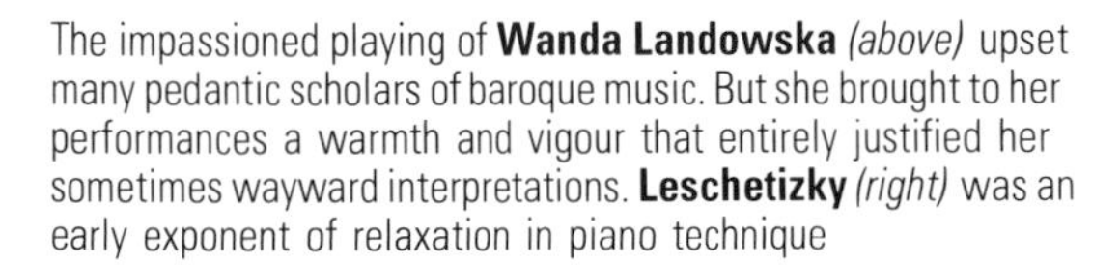

The impassioned playing of **Wanda Landowska** *(above)* upset many pedantic scholars of baroque music. But she brought to her performances a warmth and vigour that entirely justified her sometimes wayward interpretations. **Leschetizky** *(right)* was an early exponent of relaxation in piano technique

The Dutch virtuoso **Gustav Leonhardt** has made many recordings of baroque music with the recorder virtuoso, Frans Bruggen

WANDA LANDOWSKA (1879–1959)

Polish harpsichordist. Landowska was one of the first keyboard players to restore eighteenth-century music to its rightful instrument at a time when people knew little about 'period music' and even less about how to perform it. She studied at the Warsaw Conservatoire, and after an early career as a concert pianist commissioned a harpsichord from the firm of Pleyel in 1912, the first of many instruments she was to acquire. Faced with Landowska's lifetime of scholarship, pianists soon began to drop over-stuffed transcriptions of Bach and Scarlatti from their repertoires. But Landowska was at heart a Romantic; her warm and full-blooded interpretations of Bach and Scarlatti were no dry neo-classical performances, and she had a genius for underlying the dramatic and emotional content of the music. Said the great American critic Virgil Thomson: 'Landowska plays the harpsichord better than anybody else plays anything.'

She was in the process of recording two cycles of Scarlatti sonatas in Paris in 1940 when there was an attack by enemy aircraft, but she refused to stop playing. (These poignant '78' recordings, with the sound of gunfire in the background, have now been reissued as albums.) The German invasion imminent, she was shortly afterwards forced to abandon her extensive library and priceless collection of harpsichords, leaving France for the safety of Switzerland.

Two harpsichord concertos, one by Manuel de Falla, and the other, *Concert Champêtre* by Francis Poulenc, were both written for her.

ALICIA DE LARROCHA (1923...)

Spanish pianist. Alicia de Larrocha made her debut in her home town of Barcelona at the age of four. This outstanding interpreter is famed not just for her performance of Spanish keyboard music, in which field she is pre-eminent, but the whole of the piano repertoire. She is renowned for her attention to detail, nuances of expression and phrasing, and can move effortlessly from profound simplicity to passionate animation. It has been said that she scarcely ever needs to practise, and certainly her thorough knowledge of Albeniz's formidably difficult *Iberia* or Granados's *Goyescas* allows her to escape from the problems of technique to concentrate on the emotional impact of the music under her fingers. There are no more evocative performances of such works as Falla's *Nights in Gardens of Spain* than those by Alicia de Larrocha.

GUSTAV LEONHARDT (1928...)

Dutch organist and harpsichordist. He was born and spent his childhood in Amsterdam. During the German occupation the family were virtually prisoners in their own house, and for nine months the boy did not dare go outside. There were times when the family had to sleep under the floorboards while continual watch was kept at the windows. There was a harpsichord in the house, and very little else to do but play it.

After the war, Leonhardt continued his studies in Amsterdam, then went to Basle to study at the Schola Cantorum. His recital career began with his interpretation of Bach's 'Art of Fugue' on the harpsichord (Bach left no indication of which instrument(s) he intended to perform the piece). He has since recorded the cycle twice. He worked frequently with his own ensemble, known as the Leonhardt Consort, but this has now been disbanded. Leonhardt's performances of early baroque composers such as Frescobaldi, Froberger and Sweelinck are considered definitive in their field.

THEODOR LESCHETIZKY (1830–1915)

Polish pianist and teacher. As a pupil of Czerny and teacher of Schnabel, Leschetizky is the central link in a chain which stretches from Beethoven to Clifford Curzon and beyond.

In 1852 he settled in Russia, and when the St Petersburg Conservatoire opened ten years later, he obtained a teaching post there – he had already been teaching since he was fifteen. When he was nearly fifty, Leschetizky moved to Vienna, soon becoming renowned as one of the world's leading teachers of the piano. His turbulent life involved him in marriage four times (three times to pupils who were later to become celebrated pianists themselves). Of all his pupils, the most famous was undoubtedly Ignacy Paderewski.

Much has been said about the Leschetizky Method at various times. Leschetizky himself denied having any particular method, unless the avowed policy of adapting technique to serve the emotional needs or physical capabilities of the pupil could be considered a method.

JOHN LEWIS (1920...)

American pianist, composer and band leader. Lewis began piano lessons when he was seven; at university, where he later studied anthropology, he continued with music as a subsidiary subject. In 1942 he was called up for military service and met the drummer Kenny Clarke, who not only started him off on his career but later co-founded the Modern Jazz Quartet. After serving in the army, Lewis joined Dizzy Gillespie as an arranger and pianist. The MJQ, with which his name is always associated, was formed in

1951 and made its first recording in 1952. The two albums of MJQ's Stockholm concert, *European Tour*, probably contain the best music in their repertoire. Lewis's own piano style, however, may be best heard on an earlier recording, 'I can't get started' from the record *2°E, 3°W*.

The success of the MJQ can be directly attributed to Lewis's talents, especially his capacity for incorporating essentially classic forms into the context of jazz.

MEADE 'LUX' LEWIS (1905–64)

American jazz pianist. Lewis taught himself to play, mainly by watching the keys of an automatic player-piano. He got a job as a boogie player in a bar in the 1920s, when ragtime was the craze, and perfected his technique through sheer repetition of performance. When boogie became the rage round 1936 he was already an accomplished player, having made his first successful recording, the famous *Honky-Tonk Train Blues*, regarded as one of the classics of boogie. He went to New York and hit town in a big way, before being acclaimed one of the world's top three boogie players, alongside Pete Johnson and Albert Ammons.

His style stands out because of its intensity; sometimes he played quite literally 'between the cracks' with his thumb spread across two keys, while the left hand remained correspondingly light.

His interest in music began and ended with improvised piano boogie and blues; away from his instrument he seldom liked to talk about music. He was killed in a car crash in Minneapolis in 1964.

In the 1950s he recorded *Lux Flakes* with a heavy rhythm group, and was supported by a big band sound in *Camptown Races* in the early 1960s, but boogie buffs do not rate these recordings as highly as his early work.

JOSEF LHÉVINNE (1874–1944)

Russian-born American pianist. Lhévinne was a contemporary of Rachmaninov at the Moscow Conservatoire. When only fourteen he played Beethoven's *Emperor* Concerto with Anton Rubinstein conducting. He achieved several distinctions at the Conservatoire and, after obtaining his diploma, married a fellow student. For a while he taught in Tiflis and at the Moscow Conservatoire before going to the USA in 1906. There he gave a hundred concerts in a year. Following his successful marathon tour, he eventually settled in the USA after the First World War. Lhévinne's musicianship was always modest; in the most technically brilliant passages the interpretation always took precedence over showmanship. His technique, for which he had acquired a solid foundation in the Moscow Conservatoire, enabled him to play one hand octave runs with the rapidity and smoothness of a glissando.

WALTER LIBERACE (1919...)

American pianist. The son of a horn player, Liberace had a musical background, and took to the piano at an early age. He was heard and encouraged by no less a person than Paderewski, but was nevertheless inclined towards show business from his early days, playing in clubs as 'Walter Busterkeys'. He moved to New York in 1940, appeared on television, and became a popular success. While his flair for showmanship is of the highest order, there is no denying the criticism that his performances of truncated versions of the classics bear but shallow resemblance to the original: orchestral themes played on the piano, and tricky keyboard passages either shifted to the orchestra or omitted altogether. All this is set against a background of Hollywood-style lighting, dancing fountains, glittering costumes, heavy (and costly) jewellery, and the famous silver candelabra.

In spite of this ostentatious display, Liberace has shown himself to be a man of warmth and sincerity. He has helped many notable charities, and in particular has set up numerous foundations for young people of talent. His ready wit is shown in a disarming response to the query of 'Mr Liberace, how do you play with all those rings on your fingers?' His reply: 'Ve-ry well!'

DINU LIPATTI (1917–50)

Rumanian pianist and composer. In his short life, Lipatti had a tremendous influence on the people who came into contact with him. While his fame as an outstanding interpreter went round the world, Lipatti himself was only able to tour Europe before dying of rheumatoid arthritis.

He studied in Bucharest, and at the International Competition in Vienna took a second prize; Cortot, one of the judges, wanted him to have first prize and resigned from the jury in protest. He went to Switzerland in 1943, where he began to suffer from the crippling disease which was to kill him. He became a professor of the virtuoso class at the Geneva Conservatoire in 1943, and was greatly revered as a teacher. Among the many precepts which he gave his pupils was the advice to play a piece through in many different ways before starting to study it thoroughly. That way one could understand better the instrinsic argument of a piece, and come to know the end one was trying to achieve. His compositions include a concertino for piano and orchestra and a sonatina for the left hand alone. A recording of the Schumann Piano Concerto reveals the

George Malcolm has recorded the complete harpsichord works of Rameau, a composer whose music suits his own reflective temperament

excellent technique which was so soon to be extinguished. It is generally agreed that the musical world lost one of its greatest potential exponents.

RADU LUPU (1945...)

Rumanian pianist and composer. Lupu took to the piano when he felt that he was not going to succeed as a composer. He studied at the Bucharest Conservatoire and went on to take the first prize at the Leeds International Music Festival in 1969. Flattered by the obvious comparisons between himself and Dinu Lipatti, he has modestly disclaimed the technical ability. It is every pianist's right, he asserts, to be able to make mistakes, which is why he dislikes recording. His repertoire mainly incorporates Romantic music, but he is gradually introducing contemporary Rumanian composers into his programmes, as well as Bartók, whom he does not consider to be Rumanian in spirit (though Bartók's birthplace is now, geographically at least, in Rumania).

MOURA LYMPANY (1916...)

English pianist, now resident in America. Of all Moura Lympany's teachers, it was probably Tobias Matthay (with whom she studied for ten years) who has been the greatest influence. She has been an accomplished recitalist from the age of twelve, when a debut at the Harrogate Festival launched her career. One of her more interesting tours was in 1956, when she visited Russia with the London Philharmonic Orchestra under Sir Adrian Boult. She also gave the London première of Khachaturian's first piano concerto, which she took to Paris, Brussels, Milan and Vienna. She has done much to promote the cause of British music abroad, playing concertos by Rawsthorne, Arnell, Scott, Delius and Ireland.

GEORGE MALCOLM (1917...)

English harpsichordist, pianist and conductor. Although he is one of the most prominent figures in the performance of preclassical music, George Malcolm originally trained as a concert pianist. He studied at Balliol College, Oxford, and at the Royal College of Music. His first important position was as Master of the Music at Westminster Cathedral in London. He held the position from 1947 to 1959, during which time Britten composed his *Missa Brevis* for the choir. Later, with the London Symphony Orchestra and eminent soloists, they recorded Britten's *Cantata Academica*.

Malcolm's life centres round the harpsichord, even though he frequently appears as a conductor. He is usually to be heard playing at Britain's leading music festivals, either as a soloist or in ensemble, and frequently appears with other such distinguished players as Julian Bream and Yehudi Menuhin. He tours Europe and the USA regularly, and is particularly well received in Eastern Europe. In 1977 he was the first harpsichordist to make an extensive tour of Japan. George Malcolm's reputation is founded on his thorough mastery of the keyboard, extraordinary scholarship, and attention to detail which gives him a unique authority over his instruments and their music.

ARTURO BENEDETTO MICHELANGELI (1920...)

Italian pianist. One of the few Italian pianists to have made any impression internationally, Michelangeli is distinguished for his incomparable technique. He was born in Brescia and studied there before going on to the Milan Conservatoire. His first tour was after the Second World War, and he made his first appearance in London in 1946, where he created a sensation.

Sheer dexterity is matched by sensitive playing and extraordinary clarity. It is sometimes said that the emotional impact of his music is strained, and that he excels in music which is more technically demanding than soul-searching. His playing, for those who

Moscheles moved with ease in high society, and did much to make his profession accepted as a respectable one

still have ears for harpsichord music played on the piano, is exquisitely represented in his recordings of a group of Scarlatti sonatas.

THELONIOUS SPHERE MONK (1920...)

American jazz pianist and composer. Monk was one of a number of forward-looking musicians who contributed to the development of bop in the 1940s, although his style was not widely accepted for many years. He became a member of Lucky Millinder's band in 1942, when Dizzy Gillespie was part of the outfit, and in 1944 was with saxophonist Coleman Hawkins. However, he rarely played with large bands, preferring to work in trios or small combos. His greatest contribution to jazz has probably been his development of a personal harmonic style, through such pieces as *Epistrophy* and *Blue Monk*. While some critics have called him the greatest jazz composer since Duke Ellington, others have carped at his style, saying that it suffers from technical limitation. Certainly, with his coloration and piquant harmonies, Monk retains an enviable individuality.

GERALD MOORE (1899...)

English pianist. Gerald Moore has made a name for himself solely as an accompanist, but has done so to such an extent that he is often given top billing over the soloist. This is the result of a dedicated, lifelong study of the problems of accompaniment, and to a gift for being able to talk in a warm (and anecdotal) way on the elusive subject of music. His books on accompanying – *The Unashamed Accompanist* and *Am I too Loud?* are required reading for anyone entering his profession.

There is hardly an artist of international standing with whom Moore has not performed or recorded. His performances of Schubert, Schumann and Wolf *Lieder* are likely to remain definitive. Gerald Moore retired in 1967.

JELLY ROLL MORTON (1885–1941)

American jazz pianist. Morton was the greatest jazz pianist in the world – at least, according to Ferdinand Joseph la Menthe, which was Jelly Roll's real name. The pseudonym itself was a personal hymn to his prowess: as Duke Ellington said, 'Sure Jelly Roll Morton has talent . . . talent for talking about Jelly Roll Morton.' He started to play the guitar when he was seven, but took up the piano at the age of ten. He began playing in bars and brothels, and by the 1920s had achieved immense success and had a huge following largely through his recordings under the name of Morton's Red Hot Peppers from 1925-30. His flashy lifestyle, with a diamond drilled into his front teeth and his outrageously exaggerated claim to have invented jazz (in 1902!) made him a controversial figure; but by the 1930s and the onset of the Depression he had lost much of his former popularity. His unforgettable compositions include *Wolverine Blues* and *Kansas City Stomp*.

IGNAZ MOSCHELES (1794–1870)

German-Bohemian pianist, conductor and composer. Moscheles's early studies were in Prague; when his father died, he went to Vienna to study under Albrechtsberger and Salieri whilst himself working as a teacher. His career began with his performance and publication of a set of variations on a popular march, which soon became a virtual requirement in the repertoire of every pianist.

Moscheles fell between two schools: he had progressed beyond the Mozart-Clementi style, but could not approach the Chopin-Schumann era with confidence. He had great musical taste, and was always attempting to rid his concert programmes of the virtuoso-display type of composition and introduce more substantial music. He was one of the first pianists to include Beethoven's later sonatas into his repertoire.

From his comments on the music of Chopin and Schumann, which he grew to appreciate, Moscheles must have had small hands; his own technique included rapidly repeated notes, a Scarlatti-like feature which he seems to have introduced on the piano. Mendelssohn was one of his pupils, for whom Moscheles always cherished a great affection. He recognized the serious and true genius behind the public adulation of the youth, and nurtured his talents with the greatest care. They even appeared on stage together, playing two-piano music, and Mendelssohn in his turn ever afterwards spoke with reverence of Moscheles's own qualities as a musician. It is a particular tragedy that Moscheles, among virtuosos, died before the age of recording.

Crowds flocked to see **Paderewski** *(right)* for his personality as well as for his pianism. **Jelly Roll Morton** *(below)* likewise had a somewhat inflated idea of his value as a musician: he proclaimed himself the greatest pianist in the world

JOHN OGDON (1937...)

English pianist. While still a student, Ogdon played the Brahms D minor concerto under Sir John Barbirolli in 1956. He soon made a reputation as one of the most promising young British pianists, appearing at the major British festivals, including the opening night of the 'Proms' in London. In 1962 he won the Tchaikovsky Prize.

He is a giant of the keyboard both physically and intellectually – heavily built, with a warm and humorous personality. He excels in old-fashioned virtuosity: with Liszt and Rachmaninov he is in his element, and his own compositions are hardly less demanding than those Romantics he plays with such brilliance.

VLADIMIR DE PACHMANN (1848–1933)

Russian pianist. Pachmann can hardly be seriously regarded as one of the world's greatest pianists, though in his day he was certainly one of the most famous (albeit notorious) virtuosos. He attracted a middle-of-the-road audience who wanted more at their recital than mere music. George Bernard Shaw put the matter succinctly when he wrote that Pachmann 'gave his well-known pantomimic performance, with accompaniments by Chopin'. Pachmann began his recitals by going through an elaborate show of raising and lowering the piano-stool, placing perhaps a single sheet of paper on the seat, and leaning back with a satisfied sigh. He was not averse to shouting encouragement to the enthusiastic audience, or even, if he were in the audience at another's recital, climbing on to the stage to give instructions and suggestions.

He would also remain in dressing-gown and bedroom slippers to receive visitors, whatever the time of day, his excuse being that the ancient garments had once belonged to Chopin. He wore the same outfit for milking cows – a practice which, he claimed, kept his fingers supple.

IGNACY PADEREWSKI (1860–1941)

Polish pianist and statesman. One of the most famous pianists of all time

Oscar Peterson has recorded with practically every jazz player of repute for more than a quarter of a century, and has his own television series

(and certainly the most successful in financial terms), Paderewski made something like ten million dollars in fifty years – by present-day standards at least ten times that figure. He gave most of it away: most of all to his beloved Poland.

But he was not a great pianist in the sense that he could play the piano better than anyone else; his vast following was due to his magnetic personality and an astute business manager.

He was born in a country village; his mother died when he was three and his father became impoverished in the 1863 revolution. However, wealthy patrons sent him to Warsaw, where he was nearly expelled for refusing to join the Conservatoire orchestra. After graduating, he taught there for a while, then moved to Berlin for further study. In 1884 he met Leschetizky, with whom, he claimed later, he learnt more in three months than he had in twenty-four years.

In 1887 his concert career began in earnest. First he visited Vienna and Paris, then England in 1880, and America the following year. The opening series of concerts included six concertos; he had to practise for seventeen hours a day in order to tackle the schedule, but by the end of the week he was a sensation. Though critics were lukewarm, the audiences raved.

From 1910 he began to take a serious interest in Polish affairs; he gave concerts in aid of the Polish Relief Fund, visited Poland in 1910 to unveil a memorial he had commissioned, and during the First World War worked as a freelance diplomat. In 1919 he was made Prime Minister, and his signature appears accordingly on the Versailles Treaty. He retired from active music-making, devoting his attention to statesmanship and charitable works, but came out of retirement to give occasional benefit concerts.

In 1940, as President of the Polish National Council in Paris, he went to America once again to plead Poland's cause. He was never to return.

MURRAY PERAHIA (1947...)

American pianist. Perahia's first interest was opera, then the orchestra, and finally (reluctantly) the piano. Although he would go to hear concerts given by the New York Philharmonic on his own while only ten years old, he hated practising, even trying the hoary old trick of putting a record on while he sneaked out to play football. He still managed to graduate successfully from Mannes College of Music and go on to win the Leeds International Piano Competition in 1972.

His records include Chopin's piano sonatas, well suited to his fiery temperament, and the Mendelssohn piano

Maurizio Pollini *(left)* has recorded a stunning performance of the arrangement of Stravinsky's *Petrushka* for piano solo. *Below:* **Lev Pouishnoff**

concertos, recorded with the Academy of St Martin's-in-the-Fields. He has also recorded complete song cycles of Schubert, Schumann and Britten with the distinguished singer Peter Pears.

VLADO PERLEMUTER (1904...)

French pianist. He was born in Kaunas, Lithuania, to Polish parents, and had lessons from Moritz Moszkowski. At thirteen he went to the Paris Conservatoire, taking first prize in Alfred Cortot's class when only fifteen. Through Moszkowski, he came into contact with many famous artists; it was Rachmaninov who made the greatest impression on him. In 1927 Perlemuter wrote to Ravel to say that he had learnt to play all his music. Ravel was intrigued, and invited him to play, but apparently with the intention that the performances should be exact, rather than with a view to helping Perlemuter's career. Through his Polish background he became a master of Chopin. He has recorded the complete works of Ravel, and an album of Chopin pieces won the Grand Prix du Disque in 1962.

OSCAR PETERSON (1925...)

Canadian jazz pianist. Having played the piano since he was six, Peterson was spotted in a local talent contest when a teenager. From then he went on to broadcast regularly in a local radio show. In spite of tempting offers he remained in Canada until 1949, when he appeared at the Carnegie Hall. Tours and recordings brought him to the public's notice and by the mid-50s he was appearing in Boston with the singer Ella Fitzgerald.

His music grew out of swing and bop, gradually taking on a distinctive sound. He has been featured in hundreds of albums with other renowned entertainers from the musical world.

MAURIZIO POLLINI (1942...)

Italian pianist. Pollini is regarded by some critics and musicians, including Artur Rubinstein, as the greatest living pianist. He was born in Milan and studied the piano privately. He has won several international prizes, the one which set him on to his concert career being first prize at the Warsaw Chopin Competition. He tours rarely and makes few concert appearances outside Italy. His recordings of Chopin show him to be a remarkably dynamic player who interprets with technical clarity and a great sense of urgency.

LEV POUISHNOFF (1891–1959)

Russian pianist. The great virtuoso Pouishnoff toured the world after abandoning a teaching post at Tiflis in his native land. He visited the USA in 1923, and Australia and the Far East the following year. He was a great success in Iran, being the first concert pianist to appear there.

But he was best loved in Britain, where he settled after the First World War, and continued to give recitals up to the time of his death.

SVIATOSLAV RICHTER (1914...)

Russian pianist. Born in Zhitomir, Richter's first lessons were from his father. Although he gave a concert in Odessa when he was twenty, it was not until 1937 that he entered the Moscow Conservatoire to study under Heinrich Neuhaus. Gradually, rumours filtered out of the Soviet Union that there was a phenomenal pianist in Moscow. Emil Gilels, when praised, would reply, 'Ah! But you haven't heard Richter.' Stories were brought back by Western artists who had been to Moscow: Van Cliburn in 1958, and the Philadelphia Orchestra (with whom Richter had appeared as a soloist). Then one or two recordings crossed the Iron Curtain, to be followed by Richter himself.

He was forty-six when he gave his debut at Carnegie Hall. This dramatic occasion was made even more emotional by the presence in the audience of his mother, who had fled from Russia at the start of the war, and had neither seen nor dared write to her son for nearly twenty years.

The concert, at which Richter played three Beethoven sonatas, vindicated all the reports that had gone before. It was recorded, and is still available on disc. While his repertoire is one of the widest of any concert pianist, including whole collections of composers' works, he excels in middle period Beethoven. His performances of Prokofiev's sonatas are unlikely to be matched – the composer himself dedicated his ninth sonata to Richter.

LIONEL ROGG (1936...)

Swiss organist. Born and educated in Geneva, Rogg took first prize for piano and organ at the conservatoire. His first appointment was at the church of St Boniface, and since 1961 he has been professor of organ at the conservatoire

Artur Rubinstein *(right)* has written two delightful volumes of autobiography, while the critical writings of **Charles Rosen** *(below right)* are much more investigative of his art

where he studied. His recordings include two cycles of Bach's organ works, the first made in mono when he was twenty-five, and the second begun in 1970. That year he was awarded the Grand Prix du Disque for his new recording of the *Art of Fugue*. The performance was based firstly on an old Czerny edition, then with emendations based on Walcha's (Rogg's version uses much less pedal work than Walcha's). Other recordings include works by Frank Martin, his compatriot. He has composed a number of pieces, and also published teaching manuals on organ-playing and counterpoint.

CHARLES ROSEN (1927...)

American pianist and scholar. Described as an intellectual giant, able to converse on any topic from the Merovingian succession to quantum theory, Rosen made his debut as a pianist in New York in the same year that he took a degree in French literature. He is still equally at home at the keyboard or as a writer on philological and literary subjects. His book, *The Classical Style*, was hailed as one of the most significant musical treatises of the twentieth century.

Rosen can be heard in recording playing a number of works which are usually left well alone by most pianists, such as the Boulez piano sonatas, and works by Schoenberg and Webern. The more conservative may prefer his playing of the Goldberg Variations, or Beethoven's late period sonatas. But his repertoire of recordings is extensive, and includes works by Schumann, Debussy, Ravel, Bartók and Stravinsky.

MORIZ ROSENTHAL (1862–1946)

Polish pianist. A pupil of Liszt, and probably one of his most outstanding, Rosenthal made over forty recordings, providing a tangible link with the musicians of the mid-nineteenth century. Nearly all reports of his early playing say that it was brilliant, but lacking in finesse. The great critic Hanslick ventured to suggest that this would come with time, and he was right. As Rosenthal grew older, he added sensitivity to his technical prowess, poetry to oratory. In the reissues of the old Edison cylinders and later 78s, he is heard at his best in Chopin's shorter pieces, and the Liszt transcriptions of Schubert waltzes, *Soireés de Vienne*.

Rosenthal was credited with a sharp, perhaps vitriolic, wit. Among the many remarks attributed to him is one to an eternal infant prodigy: 'Tell me, how old are you still?'

ANTON RUBINSTEIN (1830–94)

Russian pianist and composer. The composer of the famous *Melody in F* is always regarded as a link between Liszt and the modern Russian Romantic school, yet Liszt never taught him; on the contrary, he seems to have been the only talented pianist that Liszt turned away. By the time he was sixteen, Rubinstein was already earning his living teaching in Vienna and Pressburg. At eighteen he moved to St Petersburg, where he studied for eight years, eventually emerging with an enormous output of compositions, including several operas. In 1854 he toured Europe to great acclaim, and settled in Paris, where he became a friend of the composer Camille Saint-Saëns.

It was said that his playing was sometimes so gentle as to move everyone to tears; at other times he would be carried away, as if his fingers were bored with having nothing to do. Another comment (whether or not intended as a criticism) was that his programmes were always very long, with as many as five Beethoven sonatas in one evening, with all the repeats, and a generous number of encores.

One of the more curious legends concerning Rubinstein was that he was an illegitimate son of Beethoven. If he was, he would have had a particularly long gestation, since Beethoven died

Schnabel *(below)* claimed the art of playing the piano lay in the pauses between the notes. **Clara Schumann** *(foot of page)* liked best to play on the pianos of Grotrian Steinweg

three years before Rubinstein was born. But people who had known the composer were often struck by the uncanny resemblance, which Rubinstein (with a good sense of publicity) did not go out of his way to deny.

ARTUR RUBINSTEIN (*c* 1889...)

American pianist. No relation to Anton Rubinstein, Artur Rubinstein was born in Poland. When his talent for music was recognized, he was sent to Berlin to study. There he made his European debut; he was later engaged as a soloist with orchestras in the major cities of Germany. Among his teachers he names Eugen d'Albert, Theodor Leschetizky, and Max Bruch, with whom he studied composition.

Rubinstein confesses that as a young man he did not apply himself seriously enough to his studies, and was able to get away with careless playing because of his fiery temperament. The pleasures of life were more important to him than practising. In 1930 he was stung by the remark that he could have been a great pianist. 'Could' was not enough, and he began to practise with fervour. He paid a second visit to America (where before he had been less favourably received) and this time was able to add virtuosity to a Romantic temperament.

Rubinstein then began a mammoth series of recordings which included what were virtually Chopin's complete works, and the major works of Brahms, Beethoven, Liszt and Schumann. His style lends itself ideally to the works of the late Romantics and impressionists, and he excels in the music of Debussy and Granados. He is probably the most recorded of any pianist, and clearly adores his work: 'Please don't tell,' he once said, '. . . but I love playing the piano so much, I would do it for nothing.'

ARTUR SCHNABEL (1882–1951)

Austrian pianist. The great Schnabel was the first to record the entire set of Beethoven Sonatas. He was a pupil of Annette Essipoff, and then her even more illustrious husband, Theodor Leschetizky. His early career centred around the usual Romantic popular composers. He visited the United States in 1921 and 1922, but was received with very little enthusiasm. It was after his performance, for the Beethoven centenary, of the whole cycle of sonatas in a series of seven Sunday concerts that he began to become well established. He repeated his success the following year with a similar *tour de force* to celebrate the Schubert centenary, and was persuaded to try another concert tour of the United States. This time he was received with acclaim – he was, perhaps, at the peak of his powers.

After his recording of the Beethoven cycle in the 1930s, Schnabel brought out a very thoroughly researched edition of Beethoven's sonatas. It must be stressed that these are very personal editions; he has altered Beethoven's marks of expression and phrasing where he thought fit, and baldly declares that he has not indicated where this is done. His accompanying notes are exemplary, but the edition is best used in association with an authentic one. He has also composed, but in a vein which owes more to the second Viennese school than to the first, melodious one.

CLARA SCHUMANN (1819–96)

German pianist. Clara Wieck was born in Leipzig and seems to have developed late as a child; she did not speak until she was four. Her father, a professional (and strict) piano teacher, taught her to play. At first she was not allowed to play the piano for more than two hours a day, afterwards she was forced to practise nothing but scales, studies and trills. She wrote sadly, some years later, that her father did not even permit her to read. By the time she was eight, she could play concertos by Mozart and Hummel. The following year Robert Schumann joined the

Willie 'The Lion' Smith's only rival for the dominant place in the Harlem piano jazz scene of the 1920s was his close friend, the great stride pianist James P. Johnson. Their two protégés, Duke Ellington and Fats Waller, were to exercise an equal dominance on the next generation of pianists

household. He was eighteen at the time, and a law student at the University, but with hopes of becoming a pianist. What began as a brotherly interest in Clara developed into love and, eventually, marriage, though in the face of violent objection from Clara's father. For much of her life, she promoted her husband's music, regularly including Schumann's music in her recital programmes. After his death at the age of 46, she always performed wearing black, in memory of her husband.

According to Leschetizky, Clara was the first pianist to play in public without music. Some regarded this as being bad form; while pianists were expected to know the music thoroughly, there was an accepted convention for having the printed note on the stand.

ALBERT SCHWEITZER (1875–1965)

Alsatian philosopher, doctor and organist. Schweitzer was renowned not only for his medical work in Equatorial Africa but for his many treatises on the music of Bach. He studied the organ with Widor, and occasionally gave recitals to raise money for his hospital in Africa. Being multilingual, he wrote his treatise *J. S. Bach, Musician and Poet* in both French and German. A theory of the book is that Bach used cryptic and other devices to express certain thoughts in music, and Schweitzer's convincing arguments were held to be unassailable for a long time. In later years, however, it has been pointed out that Bach often borrows from himself, and when he does, the same musical device is used to express different emotions. Schweitzer's performances of Bach's organ works on record have noticeably slow tempi, but a great and convincing power. He was awarded the Nobel Peace Prize in 1952.

The Mozart playing of **Rudolf Serkin** has a much larger tone than is conventional, yet it remains extraordinarily convincing

RUDOLF SERKIN (1903...)

American pianist. Born in Bohemia in 1903, Serkin studied in Vienna, one of his teachers being Arnold Schoenberg. He gave his first public performance in Vienna in 1915, and in 1920 made his debut in Berlin, playing with an orchestra conducted by Adolf Busch. His performance was so well received that for an encore he played the whole of Bach's *Goldberg Variations*. The same year he and Adolf Busch formed the duo which was to last throughout the violinist's life. Serkin first appeared in New York in 1936, and three years later settled permanently in the USA. He joined the Curtis Institute of Music, Philadelphia, and gained a very high reputation as a teacher. Serkin's playing is restless and feverish. It has been pointed out that recordings – technically accurate and altogether brilliant – are unable to capture the atmosphere, almost electrically charged, which is generated by his playing. His performance of Beethoven's *Appassionata* sonata is particularly fine, and it is worthwhile comparing his interpretations of the slow movements of Mozart concertos with those of Mozart 'specialists'.

Serkin has been awarded several honours, including the Medal of Freedom, bestowed upon him by the late President Kennedy.

GEORGE SHEARING (1919...)

English jazz pianist and composer. The blind composer of one of the best-loved jazz classics of all time, 'Lullaby of Birdland', took to playing jazz piano after hearing Fats Waller.

Playing in a jam session at a rhythm club, he was heard by the distinguished jazz lexicographer Leonard Feather, who arranged for Shearing to record in 1937 and, subsequently, to visit the United States. Much of his musical development dates from the

1940s, evolving a style that blended the piano with guitar and vibes. This distinctive sound made his group for a time one of the most popular in the United States, as well as earning him the *Melody Maker* award for best British jazz pianist seven years in succession.

CLARENCE 'PINETOP' SMITH (1904–29)

American pianist, singer and songwriter. In a short but active life, Smith was by turns a teenage tap-dancer, comedian and pianist. His life ended in a fight at Chicago's Masonic Hall, the year after he had made his first recording. It was not until six years later that his piano solo (with monologue) *Pinetop's Boogie-Woogie* became a popular number. He is regarded as the pioneer of eight-to-the-bar boogie rhythm, which was to be played by such influential jazz musicians as Count Basie and Fats Waller.

WILLIE 'THE LION' SMITH (1897–1973)

American jazz pianist. William Henry Joseph Berthol Bonaparte Bertholoff came from mixed Jewish and Negro parentage and, as his father had died when he was four, he later added the surname of his stepfather (Smith). His nickname was due to his bravery in action during the First World War. He made his first public appearance in Newark, New Jersey, and, when the war was over, went on to tour in Europe. By 1920 he had his own band in Harlem, but remained virtually unknown to the public until 1935, when he started to record regularly.

His piano technique was at once unbeatable and thoroughly individual. It ranged from a fiery stride left hand to delicate right-hand melody. His musical ability was reinforced in performance by his dynamic charm and by his skill as a raconteur. Duke Ellington, one of many great musicians who held him in respect, dedicated his *Portrait of a Lion* to Willie Smith.

SOLOMON (1902...)

English pianist. As a boy Solomon Cutner was 'discovered' by Mathilde Verne, who gave him his early training for the concert platform. He later studied in Paris, but after a short, sensational success as a young pianist of extraordinary promise, he withdrew from public appearances and spent a time in seclusion and serious study. His reappearance as a fully matured artist established his place as the foremost English pianist of his time.

His early fame was due to his interpretation of Brahms and Schubert, though these paled into insignificance beside his performances of Beethoven. Even the more familiar of these sonatas take on a new aspect in Solomon's hands. His playing has been described as austere and refined but without ever being severe.

He has not toured Europe as extensively as other artists, but is well known in Britain and America. Severe illness brought Solomon's career to a tragically early close.

T

ART TATUM (1910–56)

American jazz pianist. Born with cataracts in both eyes, Tatum was blind for most of his life. From his late teens he worked as a professional pianist, playing in night clubs and on the radio. By the mid-30s he was leading his own band, recording and gaining an international reputation. He went to London in 1938 as a soloist, and eventually formed a trio with bass and guitar.

His technique was astonishing; a light touch and an acute harmonic sense were well in advance of his contemporaries. He made several records which testify to his technique, but the quality of improvisation, which was at its best when playing with guitarist Tiny Grimes, is only hinted at in recordings. He very much impressed Artur Rubinstein, who made a point of attending his performances whenever this was possible.

CARL TAUSIG (1841–71)

Polish pianist and composer. When he was only fourteen, Tausig amazed the great Franz Liszt with his extraordinary technique. He chose to play the Chopin A♭ Polonaise, a fiendishly difficult work, well known for its repeated four notes in the left hand, played in octaves at speed. The strongest hand soon tires of the exercise, but Tausig was later to explain that his hand seemed to be built round the figure, and that he was able to play it endlessly without effort. This effortless playing was essential to Tausig; he abhorred *Spektakel*, and preferred to sit at the keyboard impassively, letting his hands do the work without any sign of physical effort. He was a pianist of quite extraordinary power, according to such authorities as Liszt and Clara Schumann, when he died of typhoid at the age of twenty-nine.

Tausig is remembered today for his arrangements of eighteenth-century music such as Bach organ fugues and Scarlatti sonatas. There is perhaps some justification in trying to emulate the symphonic sound of the organ in, say, the Bach Toccata and Fugue in D minor, but the textural thickening of Scarlatti's harpsichord sonatas robs them of their sparkle.

GEORGE THALBEN-BALL (1896…)

Australian organist. He studied at both the Royal Academy and the Royal College of Music in London. His first organist's appointment was at Holy Trinity Church, Barnes, and he occasionally took the choir from that church to hear Sir Walford Davies at the Temple Church. In 1919, owing to ill health, Sir Walford (Davies) asked Thalben-Ball to act as his deputy, and he became virtually the organist there, being officially appointed to the post four years later. His first public recital, at the Alexandra Palace, Muswell Hill, was a great success, and in 1934 he was appointed to what was then one of Britain's most prestigious organ posts – that of Organist and Curator of the Organ at the Royal Albert Hall. From 1949 he was the Civic and University Organist.

Thalben-Ball is probably Britain's best-known recital organist, and will be as familiar for his playing of popular classics such as Mendelssohn's *Wedding March* or *War March of the Priests* as for his performances of the standard organ repertoire. Many music lovers will also have heard his playing as accompanist to the boy soprano Ernest Lough's 'O for the Wings of a Dove'.

SIGISMOND THALBERG (1812–71)

Austrian pianist and composer. At one time Thalberg was regarded as the only pianist who could approach Liszt's virtuosity. But, unlike Liszt, he failed to develop his style, and as music progressed, Thalberg was left behind and eventually forgotten.

He was born in Geneva, and claimed to be the illegitimate son of noble parents. He played as a child at private parties, and then when he was thirteen, at the house of Prince Metternich. His first public appearance was in London, after which he made a successful tour of Europe in 1830.

In those days, improvisations, virtuosity and fireworks counted for more than the authentic reproduction of another composer's score, and Thalberg delighted his audiences with variations on airs from popular operas. His speciality was to play the melody line with his thumbs, decorating the outside treble and bass with arpeggios. This is familiar enough nowadays to any pianist who has played Rubinstein's *Melody in F*, but in Thalberg's day the audience would stand up to see how he achieved an effect which sounded as if three hands were playing.

Towards the end of his life, **Thalberg** *(left)* gave up music altogether. In 1863, now a very wealthy man, he settled in Italy and, for the years that remained to him, occupied himself with his vineyard there. He did not even have a piano in his home

TAMAS VASARY (1933...)

Hungarian-born Swiss pianist. Vasary began to study the piano at the age of six, and two years later performed a Mozart concerto. His studies continued under Erno Dohnányi at the Franz Liszt Academy, Budapest, and he became an assistant professor to Zoltan Kodály when he was twenty. He left Hungary during the uprising in 1956 and settled for a while in Switzerland, he and his wife taking Swiss nationality in 1972.

His career virtually began with his recordings for Deutsche Grammophon, after which, in 1961, he made his concert debuts in London and (with the Cleveland Orchestra at Carnegie Hall) in the United States. His other activities range from accompanying Dietrich Fischer-Dieskau and two-piano work with Peter Frankl to an increasing number of commitments as a conductor. His activities in this field have been mainly in Britain.

HELMUT WALCHA (1907...)

German organist and harpsichordist. Walcha was born and studied in Leipzig, then moved to Frankfurt in 1929 (where he has been professor at the Music Institute and organist at the Dreikönigskirche). Being blind from boyhood has naturally made profound difficulties for the career of a virtuoso, and he has left Frankfurt rarely. He studies new pieces with the help of his wife, who plays the music over phrase by phrase until it is memorized. She also assists him with the registration, and sometimes (according to a distinguished critic) the pedalling as well.

His approach to the music of Bach has been greatly influenced by Schweitzer's own style. His playing can be heard on a superb Ruckers harpsichord in a recording of the first book of the '48', but it may be noticed that, as with Schweitzer, the tempi are on the slow side.

THOMAS 'FATS' WALLER (1904–43)

American jazz pianist, organist and composer. Waller was a professional pianist by the time he was fifteen (although his clergyman father had wanted him to follow in his footsteps) and by the time he was twenty he was already accompanying such great singers as Bessie Smith. His gift for jazzing-up ordinary commercial songs made him a success with audiences and colleagues alike; perhaps the most outstanding example was his treatment of 'I'm Gonna Sit Right Down and Write Myself A Letter'. To the public he presented an image of clown and entertainer, but deep down he had a serious nature – much of his spare time was spent in playing Bach's music on the organ. Of his own songs, 'Ain't Misbehavin' ' and 'Honeysuckle Rose' have become established standards. At his death he was at the height of his success, having recorded over five hundred pieces.

Fats Waller *(above)* had a generosity of spirit and a humility that made him beloved by all who knew him. On one occasion when he was playing in a nightclub, the pianist **Art Tatum** *(left)* was in the audience. Waller stopped playing, and went to the microphone: 'Ladies and gentlemen,' he said, 'I play the piano, but God is in the house tonight.' Tatum's technique was unapproachable, at least by other jazz pianists. The formidable virtuoso Godowsky was a great fan of his playing. His particular style depended up to a point on complex right-hand flourishes, not unlike the ornamentation of the baroque period, though highly personal

Waller's personal habits were to cut short his life; stories abound of his supposed ability to eat twenty hamburgers at a sitting, and by his mid-twenties he was an alcoholic.

GLOSSARY

ARPEGGIO. The notes of a chord played separately and in sequence, either as a melodic figure or as an accompaniment.

ATONAL. Having no tonal centre or 'key' to which the music gravitates. Atonality is a feature of certain schools of twentieth-century composition.

CADENZA. A passage in a concerto or aria specifically for the soloist to display his technical skill. In early concertos (e.g. Mozart's) the cadenzas are improvised. Later composers (e.g. Grieg) wrote out their cadenzas in full.

CANON. An academic musical device (met with more frequently than might be supposed) in which one voice or instrument begins a melody, followed by another voice or instrument beginning the same melody before the first has finished. Children's rounds, such as *Three Blind Mice,* are the best-known examples of canon.

CHOIR ORGAN. In a three-manual organ, the manual nearest the player which operates the quieter stops suitable for accompanying the choir.

CHROMATIC. A term used to refer to notes in a passage of music which do not belong to its key, for example the use of any of the black notes in a passage of music in C major. Music which contains a high proportion of notes foreign to the key (accidentals) could be described as highly chromatic.

CLAVIER (*also* Klavier). A German term signifying any keyboard instrument (though it only rarely includes the organ). It also refers to the manual of the instrument, as in 'Pour clavecin à deux claviers' ('For harpsichord with two manuals').

CONCERTO. Usually, a work for soloist and orchestra, but occasionally for more than one, as in Mozart's Concerto for Two Pianos and Orchestra. Unusual uses of the term are Bach's Italian Concerto (a concerto grosso for solo harpsichord) and Bartók's Concerto for Orchestra, which has no soloist.

COUNTERPOINT. Music in which two or more lines of melody are combined together, as distinct from ordinary harmony, where there is a theme with subordinate accompaniment. It is possible to have harmony without counterpoint, but all counterpoint implies some form of harmony.

DIAPASON. The main rank of pipes in an organ, distinctive in tone and shape. They are cylindrical, and generally made of a tin or zinc alloy.

DIATONIC. A term referring to music built from the conventional seven-note scale (major or minor), as distinct from music which is serial, atonal or in any other way exotic or experimental.

DYNAMICS. The distinction between the loudness and quietness in a piece of music, whether controlled by the player's hands or by the stops of the instrument.

FORTEPIANO. The forerunner of the piano, light in string tension because of its wooden frame, and with leather-covered hammers that give a clear, distinctive tone.

FUGUE. A highly complex composition, in which lines of melody are combined in accordance with accepted rules. Regarded as the supreme test of a composer's craftsmanship, a fugue may be academically correct and yet dull, but in the hands of a master of the form, such as Bach or Mozart, it can display the composer's extraordinary creative genius.

GREAT ORGAN. The main body of the organ, played from the central manual in a three-manual instrument or the lower manual in one with two keyboards.

IMPROMPTU. In the strict sense, a piece which is improvised, but more usually a piece composed in a quasi-improvisatory style.

IMPROVISATION. The art of composing spontaneously while playing. Until the late nineteenth century, all performers were expected to show some proficiency at improvisation, though the practice today is virtually confined to the fields of organ-playing and jazz.

LEGATO. A smooth style of playing that avoids audible gaps between notes or ungainly breaks in the phrasing. The cultivation of an expressive legato is a desideratum of every aspiring pianist.

MANUAL. The keyboard of an organ or harpsichord, a term used particularly to distinguish the manuals from the pedalboard.

MODAL. Technically, belonging to one of the ancient Church, rhythmic or folksong modes, but more commonly applied to a style of music which has a tonal centre but cannot be defined as major or minor. Modal music is usually encountered before 1700, and occasionally after 1850.

OPUS. From the Latin *'work'*. Opus numbers are often the most precise means of identifying a composer's works, and usually indicate the order in which the pieces have been published or composed. *Op. posth.* indicates that the work was published posthumously, and consequently may have been a late work or one recently discovered. The term came into general use about the time of Beethoven.

OVERTURE. In baroque music, two kinds of overture predominated: Italian and French. The former is rare in Keyboard Music, but the French Overture is found frequently in the works of Bach and Handel. It is distinguished by having a stately introduction followed by a more rapid-moving fugal section.

PARTITA. Originally a set of variations. By the high baroque period, the term had come to be synonymous with 'suite'.

PASSACAGLIA. A dance form, originally in triple time, and characterized by the use of a ground bass.

PEDAL ORGAN. The keyboard of an organ or harpsichord that is played with the feet. It operates the lowest notes of the instrument. By extension, the term 'pedal' has come to mean a long, held note in the bass, even in piano music, where it has to be held by the hands alone.

PEDALLING. In piano music, the term refers to the use of the sustaining (right-hand) pedal to enrich the overall harmony of a passage, or to join parts of a musical phrase which would otherwise be disconnected when the hands change position. In organ music, it refers to the use of the pedal-organ.

PROGRAMME MUSIC. The term applies to music that is deliberately descriptive of an extra-musical event. It may portray a mood, or even set out to tell a story.

QUILL. The plucking of a harpsichord has traditionally been done by such quills as those of the raven. In later ages leather and even nylon have been employed.

RANK. In an organ or harpsichord, the term refers to all the pipes or strings of a particular tone colour.

RONDO. A musical form in which repetitions of a theme are interspersed with episodes. There is also sonata-rondo form, which uses more than one theme and characteristically develops them with more complexity.

RUBATO. From the Italian 'robbed'. It refers to judicious variations in the tempo of a piece that is being performed. Often, the left-hand accompaniment may retain a constant tempo in its figuration while the right hand, playing the melody, slows down for added expression and then has to catch up again. Chopin's Nocturnes are a well-known vehicle for excessive *tempo rubato.*

SONATA. Literally, an instrumental composition, as opposed to *cantata*, a vocal one. More specifically, it is applied to a musical structure which flourished between 1760 and 1850 (see p. 54). Classically, a sonata has four movements, though variants are common.

SONATINA. A short sonata, often technically undemanding.

STOP. The means by which the various ranks of the organ or harpsichord are brought into play. On an organ they might be in the form of heavy drawstops, or touch-sensitive tabs that are electrically operated. On the harpsichord they are usually small knobs which need to be moved only a fraction of an inch to bring the rank into play, but occasionally foot-operated pedals may serve the same purpose.

SUITE. An extended work, made up chiefly of dance movements. Centred around the allemande, courante, sarabande and gigue, suites were often preceded by a substantial prelude and interspersed with other dances, such as minuets, bourrées, gavottes, etc.

SWELL. A organ device for shading the dynamics by enclosing the pipes in a large cabinet. This is fitted with slats that can be opened or closed by the performer operating a pedal: the slats resemble a Venetian blind. A similar device was used in the latter days of the harpsichord, when it was trying to compete with the pianoforte.

INDEX

Compiled by Audrey Twine

Page numbers in bold type (**12**) indicate biographical sections and important references. *Italic* page numbers (*12*) direct the reader to illustrations or their captions.

H

I

J

K

L

Q

R

S

T

V

W

ACKNOWLEDGEMENTS

GENERAL ACKNOWLEDGEMENTS

The author and publishers would like to thank the following for their invaluable help in compiling this book: Ruth Hall, whose piano (featured on the jacket) has withstood the study of all the pieces mentioned in *Keyboard Instruments*, Derek Walters, Maggie Colbeck, Jonathan Gill-Skelton, Richard Burgess-Ellis and John Beresford Slinger. Especial gratitude is also due to Cordelia Chitty and George Reynolds for their advice and support throughout the project.

ARTISTS CREDITS

Jeremy Alsford (Studio Briggs Ltd) 19, 22, 23, 26, 27
Jeremy Banks (Studio Briggs Ltd) Prelims Artwork
Peter Morter 20, 21, 24, 25, 28, 29

Jacket photograph by **Peter Loughran**

PICTURE CREDITS

A: above; C: centre; B: below; L: left; R: right.

8: Deutsche Grammophon; 11: Encyclopédie-Lutherie; 12–13: National Gallery, London; 14–15: BBC Hulton Picture Library; 16–17: BBC Hulton Picture Library; 18(AR, CR): Mansell Collection; 18–19: Photo: Hugh J Sykes, reproduced by courtesy of the Henley and District Organ Trust; 19(AL): Cooper-Bridgeman Library; 20(BL): BBC Hulton Picture Library; 22(AR): Barnabys Picture Library; 23(A,C): Royal College of Music; 23(CR): R L Mitchell/Morley Galleries, London; 26(L): Mansell Collection; 27(AL,CL): R L Mitchell/Morley Galleries, London; 30: Bodleian Library, Oxford; 32: Mansell Collection; 33(A): By permission Viscount De L'Isle, VC, KG, from his collection at Penshurst Place, Kent; 33(B): Mary Evans Picture Library; 34: Royal College of Music; 35(CL): Royal College of Music; 35(BR): Fitzwilliam Museum, Cambridge; 36(CL): Gemeente Museum, The Hague; 36(BL): BBC Hulton Picture Library; 37: National Portrait Gallery, London; 38: Mansell Collection; 39: Bildarchiv Preussischer Kulturbesitz; 40(CL): Bildarchiv Preussischer Kulturbesitz; 40–41: Bulloz; 42: Royal College of Music; 43: Giraudon; 44: Royal College of Music; 46–47: Bildarchiv Preussischer Kulturbesitz; 48: National Portrait Gallery, London; 49: Scala; 50(L,C,R): Archiv für Kunst und Geschichte; 51(A): National Portrait Gallery, London; 51(B): BBC Hulton Picture Library; 52(AL): Archiv für Kunst und Geschichte; 52(CL): Amt der Bur Genländischen; 52–53: ZEFA: Archiv für Kunst und Geschichte; 54–55: Archiv für Kunst und Geschichte; 56(CL): Archiv für Kunst und Geschichte; 56(BL): The British Library; 56–57: Royal College of Music; 58: Archiv für Kunst und Geschichte; 60: Bulloz/Petit Palais; 63: Royal College of Music; 64: Bulloz; 66(L): Royal College of Music; 66(R): Mary Evans Picture Library; 68–69: Bildarchiv Preussischer Kulturbesitz; 69(C): Royal College of Music; 69(BR): Bildarchiv Österreichische Nationalbibliothek; 71: Royal College of Music; 72(AL): The Bettmann Archive; 72(AR): Novosti Press Agency; 72(BR): René Dazy; 74–75: Society for Cultural Relations with the USSR; 76(AL): Novosti Press Agency; 76–77: Ampliaciones y Reproducciones MAS; 77(AR): Cooper-Bridgeman Library; 78(A): Nadar/© Arch. Photo: Paris/SPADEM; 78(B): Giraudon/©SPADEM; 79: Roger-Viollet; 81(A,B): BBC Hulton Picture Library; 82–83: BBC Hulton Picture Library; 83(R): Universal Edition (Alfred A. Kalmus) Limited; 84(A): Embassy of the Hungarian Peoples Republic, London; 84(B): Novosti Press Agency; 85(L): David Redfern Photography; 85(R): Library of Congress; 87(AL): Performing Arts Services Inc.; 87(AR): Erich Auerbach; 87(B): Elizabeth Photo Library; 88: Phonogram International; 89: Deutsche Grammophon; 90(AC): Val Wilmer; 90(CR): Royal College of Music; 91: Royal College of Music; 92: Fox Photos; 93(A): Royal College of Music; 93(B): IBBS and Tillett Ltd; 94(A): Royal College of Music; 94–95: Clive Barda; 95(BR): Val Wilmer; 97(A,B): Royal College of Music; 98(A): CBS Records; 98(B): Royal College of Music; 100: Classical Music Weekly; 102(A): Deutsche Grammophon; 102(BL,BR): Royal College of Music; 103 Brandt/h.m. Archiv; 105: IBBS and Tillett Ltd; 106: Royal College of Music; 107(A): Royal College of Music: 107(B): Val Wilmer; 108: Val Wilmer; 109(A): Deutsche Grammophon; 109(B): Royal College of Music; 110(AR): Clive Barda; 110(CR): CBS Records; 111(CR): Courtesy of EMI Records Limited; 111(BR): Royal College of Music; 112: Val Wilmer; 113: Clive Barda; 114(A): Royal College of Music; 114–15 *Melody Maker*; 115: Courtesy of EMI Records Limited